MOMENTS
of IMPACT

HOW TO DESIGN STRATEGIC CONVERSATIONS
THAT ACCELERATE CHANGE

Chris Ertel and Lisa Kay Solomon

SIMON & SCHUSTER

New York London Toronto Sydney New Delhi

Simon & Schuster
1230 Avenue of the Americas
New York, NY 10020

First Simon & Schuster hardcover edition February 2014

SIMON & SCHUSTER and colophon are registered trademarks of Simon & Schuster, Inc.

For information about special discounts for bulk purchases,
please contact Simon & Schuster Special Sales at
1-866-506-1949 or business@simonandschuster.com.

The Simon & Schuster Speakers Bureau can bring authors to your live event.
For more information or to book an event contact the Simon & Schuster Speakers
Bureau at 1-866-248-3049 or visit our website at www.simonspeakers.com.

Jacket design by MINE, www.minesf.com

Manufactured in the United States of America

10 9 8 7 6 5 4 3 2 1

Library of Congress Cataloging-in-Publication Data

Ertel, Chris.
  Moments of impact : how to design strategic conversations that accelerate
change / Chris Ertel and Lisa Kay Solomon.
    pages   cm
    1. Leadership. 2. Public speaking. I. Solomon, Lisa Kay. II. Title.
HM1261.E78 2014
303.3'4—dc23   2013031453

ISBN 978-1-4516-9762-9
ISBN 978-1-4516-9769-8 (ebook)

For ambitious leaders everywhere who want to make a difference,
one conversation at a time

CONTENTS

THE MOST IMPORTANT LEADERSHIP SKILL THEY DON'T TEACH AT HARVARD BUSINESS SCHOOL

(OR ANYWHERE ELSE)

The call came eight days before the meeting. The caller—let's call him Bruce—was anxious. A senior executive at an international development agency, Bruce was about to host one of the biggest meetings of his career. Forty top economic-development experts from around the world were coming to Jakarta—on his invitation—to strategize about the future of Asia. As the date approached, Bruce was petrified that the two-day session might flop.

We asked him a few questions: What's the purpose of the meeting? What are the desired outcomes? "We just want people to come and talk, so they can learn from one another," Bruce said. "After all, they're the experts."

What important points do your experts already agree on? Where are they at loggerheads? "We figured we'd sort that out in the room. We haven't had time to talk with everyone in advance."

How will you set up the issues? "We've got a list of eight priority topics on the agenda. We figured we'd work through them one at a time with the group."

What kind of environment are you creating to help them be productive? "The meeting is in a big hotel near the center of town. I haven't been there yet, but you can check out their website. It looks pretty nice."

What kind of overall experience are you hoping participants will have? "Er, what do you mean by that, exactly?"

As we peppered Bruce with more questions—Who's kicking off the meeting and what will he or she say? What kinds of insights and next steps do you want people to walk away with?—we could feel his stress level rise. Bruce hadn't thought through some basic but critical stuff. Now, his time was running out.

We shifted into triage mode to figure out what might be done in the little time remaining. Bruce had another idea. "Can you be in Jakarta on Monday?"

DESIGNING STRATEGIC CONVERSATIONS: A CRAFT, NOT A CRAPSHOOT

Bruce is an accomplished professional with a top-notch education and years of experience running meetings and events. Yet at no point in his career did he learn how to design a gathering like the one he was about to host—a creative, collaborative problem-solving session tackling a messy, open-ended challenge. That's not a garden-variety meeting. That's a *strategic conversation*.

If you're a manager on the rise or a leader in your organization today, you've no doubt been to or organized at least a few strategic conversations. At some point, virtually all leaders—at all levels, across all organizations—convene them to address their most vexing challenges. At these critical moments, everyone will be looking to *you*—not for all the answers, but to help *them* unearth answers together.

Odds are, you have some ideas on how to set up a strategic conversation—but less than total confidence in how to get great results. Most leaders approach strategic conversations with a degree of anxiety because it's a skill they were never taught. To our knowledge, no major business school or executive education program includes a course (or even a module) on how to design them.

Think about it. We go to great lengths and expense to bring together our best talent, with different skills and backgrounds, to tackle our biggest challenges. Yet we have precious little guidance on how to do this well—either as participants or as leaders.

It's a bizarre oversight. Imagine if a professional golfer trained for all parts of the game—except putting. She can hit 250-yard drives straight down the fairway and chip with precision, only to stumble around the green. A pro golfer wouldn't last long without the ability to putt. How can any leader expect to get far without the ability to spark productive collaboration around critical challenges?

Because we pay little attention to this skill, every day an otherwise capable leader is hosting a strategy retreat without a clear purpose. Or a strategic planning session packed with presentations that lay out one fact after another without illuminating the choices at hand. Or a feel-good off-site where participants are asked to give their "input" though it's obvious the leaders have already made up their minds. Or a freewheeling brainstorm session where "every idea is good." We could go on and on. But so could you, we suspect.

Even when we get the basics right, things can still fall flat. The right people are in the room, the question is clear, the content is pretty good, and yet . . . somehow, not much happens. People talk around the issues but make no progress. In our work, this is known as *slipping clutch syndrome*. You think you've got the car in drive, but it keeps falling back into neutral.

Bruce's meeting in Jakarta went "okay," we later found out. The experts kicked around a few interesting ideas and made some new networking connections. But the energy level never took off. There was no follow-through. Afterward, people grabbed their bags, caught flights home, and that was the end of it. Bruce had his chance to be a hero at a key moment. Instead, he was just exhausted.

Lots of strategic conversations turn out "okay"—neither home runs nor disasters. But okay strategic conversations are *not* okay. They carry an immense price. They waste precious time and money—in some settings, well into the hundreds of thousands of dollars. They de-motivate participants and make them wonder if leaders know what they're doing. Worst of all, they can lead to terrible decisions that put careers or entire organizations in jeopardy.

By contrast, great strategic conversations can be powerful *moments of impact* that drive positive change in an organization. They generate novel insights by combining the best ideas of people with different backgrounds and perspectives. They lift participants above the fray of daily concerns and narrow self-interest, reconnecting them to their greater, collective purpose. And they lead to deep, lasting changes that can transform an organization's future. We've seen it happen many times, often against the odds.

Yet the difference between an okay strategic conversation and a moment of impact isn't random luck. Designing strategic conversations is a craft—not a crapshoot. It's a craft defined by a few core principles and key practices that can catapult a "been there, done that" meeting into a gathering that few will forget.

Moments of Impact is a book with a mission. We want to eradicate as many time-sucking, energy-depleting strategy meetings as possible—and replace them with inspiring and productive strategic conversations. We aim to deliver the single most useful resource for managers and leaders who need better strategic conversations—now—to shape the future of their organizations for the better.

NEIL GRIMMER'S MOMENT OF IMPACT

Neil Grimmer is passionate about healthy food—especially when it comes to his two little girls. Grimmer is cofounder, CEO, and "Chief Dad" of Plum Organics, a baby-food company launched in 2007 with the goal of transforming the way small kids eat. The company offers sustainable, organic food (featuring unusual ingredients such as purple carrots) in innovative packaging, such as resealable pouches imported from Japan. By 2011, Plum Organics had built a loyal customer base, with annual revenues approaching $40 million.

In early 2012, Grimmer felt that his business was at an inflection point.

Other small competitors with similar approaches were popping up, threatening to crowd the market. Meanwhile, Plum had hit the radar screen of big market leaders such as Gerber and Beech-Nut. "Most of our gains so far had come from their losses," says Grimmer. "But you can only squeeze so much shelf space away from big players before they take notice and respond."[1]

Grimmer knew it was time to engage his board in a strategic conversation. Its five members—all successful entrepreneurs or major investors—had many more years of experience navigating tricky competitive waters than he did. He needed their advice and guidance. But to get it, he knew he had to take a different approach from what he had done in the past. "We had talked about the what-ifs of competition before, but it had always been theoretical and elusive," says Grimmer. "This time, we needed a more action-oriented discussion."

At this critical point, most leaders would have reached for traditional business planning and strategy tools. Instead, Grimmer—a sculptor and designer by training—got creative. Rather than subjecting his board to the usual dense presentations and reports on Plum's top competitors (which they'd seen before anyway), he came up with a war-gaming exercise designed to shake things up.

With just two hours on a standing meeting agenda, Grimmer paired each board member with a Plum team member and assigned each duo the role of a Plum competitor. For the first hour, he tasked each pair to do some web-based research and come up with a plan to present to the larger group. Their assignment: find a way to steal Plum's small but growing market share. To set the right tone, Grimmer introduced the activity with a slide that had just three words—"Baby Food Fight!"—and an image of a cute baby waving boxing gloves.

Going into the session, Grimmer was apprehensive. As a former consultant, he thought the odds of success were good. But as CEO, he was less sure how his board members would respond to their unusual assignment. "My instinct was to provide them with detailed background materials,"

Grimmer says. "But instead we asked them to do the primary research themselves, which they could have rejected. Unless they entered the exercise with the right spirit, it could have been lame."

Grimmer needn't have worried. The teams dove into the assignment. Because everyone could see the other teams hard at work, a sense of competition kicked in. At one point, Grimmer noticed that two teams had come together. The pair representing private-label brands was conspiring with the duo representing a niche player similar to Plum.

When the larger group reconvened, these two combined teams unveiled a dramatic plot to dominate the organic baby-food market: capture both the higher and lower ends with a one-two punch, using separate brands but the same supply chain and distribution networks.

"From a theatrical standpoint, all of a sudden, everyone *felt* the competition," Grimmer recalls. "It became visceral. At that moment, we felt as if we were at a board meeting of our competitor. After that, the other players also got in character and raised their game."

In the end, the results exceeded Grimmer's expectations. "We came away with radical alignment that would not have happened otherwise," he says. The exercise made clear the key challenges ahead for Plum—and what they might do to position the company against rising competition. Board members also left the session with a stronger shared understanding of the competitive dynamics at play. In the months that followed, it became clear that Plum needed to expand internationally to bolster its position. In early 2013, it acquired a British company with a similar approach and coincidental name: Plum UK.

To date, Plum continues to grow at a strong pace despite a crowded field, with combined revenues over $90 million in 2012. In mid-2013, the company was sold to Campbell's Soup Company.[2] While many factors contributed to Plum's success, the Baby Food Fight was a moment of impact that helped propel the organization in a positive direction.

The Baby Food Fight worked for a number of reasons. It worked because it engaged board members in active problem-solving rather than asking them to lean back and judge the work of the management team. It worked because it ignited the passions and emotions of participants. And it worked because Grimmer was willing to take a few well-placed risks—knowing that a business-as-usual approach wouldn't cut it.

Grimmer's approach didn't require a lot of props, tons of data, or advanced facilitation skills. It just required a dash of creativity and courage—and, most important, a shift in mind-set.

STRATEGIC CONVERSATIONS: THE THIRD WAY

Faced with a tough challenge that calls for collaboration—such as increasing competitive pressures or a shift in business models—most leaders will reach for one of two well-worn devices: the standard meeting or the brainstorming session. While both are fine for many situations, neither is sufficient for dealing with messy, open-ended challenges.

As Patrick Lencioni points out in his provocative *Death by Meeting*, most standard meetings fail to deliver the all-in participation that's required to wrestle with tough issues.[3] They invite participants to play out their established roles while multitasking on the side. And according to Keith Sawyer, a psychology professor who specializes in the study of creativity, brainstorming has a poor track record in delivering results. "Decades of research have consistently shown that brainstorming groups think of far fewer ideas than the same number of people who work alone and later pool their ideas," he writes.[4]

There has to be another option—and, thankfully, there is. Strategic conversations are the third way. A strategic conversation doesn't feel like a regular meeting or a brainstorming session. It is its own distinct type: an interactive strategic problem-solving session that engages participants not just analytically but creatively and emotionally.

Strategic conversations happen in lots of places. They're not the exclusive domain of corporate strategy or strategic planning departments. They can take place in formal or informal settings—from a board meeting to a casual retreat. They can be workshops, working sessions, or a module within a regular meeting. Most of the time, they involve at least five to ten people and at least half a day. Their defining features are that the stakes are high, the answers unclear, and the participants are expected to create real insights together—rather than play out prepared scripts—across organizational boundaries.

Here are a few examples of the kinds of open-ended, high-stakes situations that call for strategic conversations:

▸ *A product development team trying to find "the next big thing" for its customers.*

▸ *An HR executive wanting to engage the organization in crafting a talent strategy.*

▸ *A management team trying to understand how global forces could affect their industry and markets.*

▸ *A school planning committee trying to decide what infrastructure and staff to put in place for the future, with limited resources.*

▸ *A business unit leader looking for ways to expand in a slow-growth environment.*

▸ *A start-up's leadership team facing a "pivot or persevere" decision point around its business model.*

▸ *An IT department head trying to define a new technology platform to support diverse parts of the organization.*

Many people feel their organizations have too many damn meetings already. They're probably right. But we suspect those same organizations don't have nearly enough strategic conversations—especially for the times we live in.

WELCOME TO "VUCA WORLD"

While it may be cliché to note that the world is changing fast these days, that doesn't make it any less true. Unforeseen turbulence has become such a constant feature in our world that military planners (among others) have an official term for it. They call it VUCA World—an environment of nonstop volatility, uncertainty, complexity, and ambiguity.[5]

VUCA World is a bit like an amusement park: it's full of thrilling rides—just not all of them are fun. It's a world where stock prices swing wildly from one week to another and entire industries become features in larger ecosystems. A world where new competitors pop up out of nowhere and disruptive technologies wipe out entrenched business models overnight. A world where a political coup or a tsunami on the other side of the planet can disrupt markets in surprising ways.

Pure Digital Technologies—the makers of Flip Video—offers a vivid example of how market directions can shift in VUCA World. Two entrepreneurs—working out of a small office above a jewelry store in downtown San Francisco—set out to create an ultra-cheap video recorder that anyone could use. The first mass-market Flip camera, which could upload videos directly by USB drive, came out in 2007. It cost a bit over $100 and became the top-selling camcorder on Amazon.com within weeks of its launch.

For the next few years, Flip owned the category of low-end camcorders, despite being copied by giants such as Sony. Flip used its small scale to churn out incremental innovations—such as high-definition quality and customizable "skins"—faster than large incumbents, while maintaining a low price tag. In March 2009, Cisco Systems acquired Pure Digital Technologies for $590 million.[6]

Just two years later, in April 2011, Cisco closed down Flip Video and sold off the remaining inventory at a deep discount. By then, low-cost video was becoming a ubiquitous feature inside mobile phones and cameras. Cisco also shifted its strategy away from consumer products, deciding to focus on its core business in enterprise markets.

That's how fast change can happen today: a new company can come out of nowhere and move from scrappy start-up to market dominance to a massive payday and then back to oblivion *in just four years.* In VUCA World, organizations face constant surprises from all directions. By the time you think you've got an important market trend figured out, it's already moved on.

ADAPTIVE CHALLENGES CALL FOR ADAPTIVE LEADERSHIP

Ronald Heifetz has been a popular teacher on leadership at Harvard Kennedy School for more than two decades. In a series of fine books, Heifetz and his colleagues draw a distinction between technical and adaptive challenges that's critical to understand in navigating VUCA World. It's foundational to our approach to strategic conversations.[7]

Technical challenges involve applying well-honed skills to well-defined problems—such as building a bridge or organizing a production line. Technical challenges may be complex, but they can still be resolved within well-understood boundaries. In these situations, more traditional, hierarchal approaches to leadership work well. If you're having heart surgery, you want the most experienced surgeon calling the shots—not a consensus-building exercise.

Adaptive challenges, by contrast, are messy, open-ended, and ill defined. In many cases, it's hard to say what the right question is—let alone the answer. Many of the most important strategic challenges that organizations wrestle with today are adaptive challenges, such as the ones we listed earlier.

It's nearly impossible for any one senior executive—or small leadership team—to solve adaptive challenges alone. They require observations and insights from a wide range of people who see the world and your organization's problems differently. And they require combining these divergent perspectives in a way that creates new ideas and possibilities that no individual would think up on his or her own.

Navigating and solving adaptive challenges demands a different set of leadership muscles—such as asking penetrating questions, winning the full engagement of colleagues, and connecting insights from different sources in real time. While some leaders develop these skills over time, they're rarely the focus of business school programs or annual performance reviews. Because these skills are less familiar, leaders often try to analyze their way through adaptive challenges instead. They grab at "silver bullet" technical approaches that address only part of the challenge, if that.

WHITHER STRATEGY?

Given the realities of VUCA World, many leaders today are wary of traditional tools for strategy, which were built largely for tackling technical challenges during more stable times. These days, the notion of three- or five-year strategic plans with their predictable, incremental improvements feels quaint—more like a relic of the Soviet era than a leading practice of a dynamic, modern business. Henry Mintzberg made this observation back in 1994 with his seminal work, *The Rise and Fall of Strategic Planning.*[8] Today, though many organizations still run annual strategic planning cycles, it's often a check-the-box exercise that helps coordinate activities but produces few novel insights.

Meanwhile, the idea of a corporate grand strategy as a source of sustainable competitive advantage is also losing ground. The oft-cited examples of coherent, durable, and successful corporate strategies are so familiar— Southwest Airlines, Apple, Enterprise Rent-A-Car—precisely because they're so rare. While the idea of setting an enduring strategic direction still has strong appeal, it's tough to do when the playing field keeps shifting and the goalposts won't stop moving.

Still, most organizations feel obliged to keep up appearances by putting out official strategies and plans. As the cubicle-dwelling cartoon figure Dilbert knows, such documents often consist of either generic statements ("Delight our customers," "Grow share in our target markets," or that old chestnut "Maximize shareholder value") or a laundry list of current initiatives ("Increase net promoter scores by 5 percent," "Reduce waste across the supply chain")—or both. Their purpose may be more to reassure employees and investors that someone is awake at the wheel than to provide real guidance for decision-making. Strategies like these remind us of a Hollywood set of an old Western town. It looks good from the outside, so long as you don't push too hard on it.

Richard Rumelt is a professor at UCLA's Anderson School of Management who's been writing, teaching, and consulting about strategy for four decades. His recent book *Good Strategy/Bad Strategy* provides a sweeping overview of strategy today. It's not pretty. As Rumelt observes:

> *Unfortunately, good strategy is the exception, not the rule. And the problem is growing. More and more organizational leaders say they have a strategy, but they do not. Instead, they espouse what I call bad strategy. Bad strategy tends to skip over pesky details such as problems. It ignores the power of choice and focus, trying instead to accommodate a multitude of conflicting demands and interests. Like a quarterback whose only advice to teammates is "Let's win," bad strategy covers up its failure to guide by embracing the language of broad goals, ambition, and values.*[9]

THE RISE OF THE "HYPHENATED STRATEGISTS"

Still, strategy isn't dying—it's evolving. If strategy was like a high-stakes chess game a few decades ago, it's more like hockey today—fast, risky, and hard to follow. There's at least as much improvisation as there is planning involved.

At the corporate level, company leaders tend to set broad direction and then expect to deal with a shifting menu of issues rather than lay out a detailed agenda for years to come. Meanwhile, leaders and managers across the organization are being hit with waves of adaptive challenges at all levels, making more decisions under uncertain conditions and with limited guidance.

Strategy is thus a pervasive and fluid activity in most organizations today, with key issues and opportunities popping up in different parts of the organization at different times, calling for a host of different approaches. While few executives feel comfortable admitting out loud that this is how strategy really happens, it may be the only realistic way to navigate the relentless challenges of VUCA World.

As a result, a flowering of "hyphenated strategists" has emerged—people with the word *strategic* in their title, such as strategic marketing director, strategic product development, strategic ventures, and so on. We suspect that most large organizations today have far more hyphenated strategists than people in central strategy offices, which tend to be lean and mean when they exist at all.

Amid all this flux and change, there is one constant. If you want to make progress against adaptive challenges, you have to harness the best thinking and judgment of your best people—especially when they don't agree. The old saying is true: nobody is as smart as all of us. Plus, it's a lot harder to put strategic decisions into action if the people executing them aren't part of the conversation.

Leaders thus face a world-class dilemma: they need to make good strategic choices under uncertainty while engaging more people with different perspectives, more effectively, in the process—*and* do it all faster, too. To do this well, we've got to put the people back into strategy—in a much smarter way. Today, more than ever, strategy *is* the conversation.

WHERE WE'RE COMING FROM

We've spent the past fifteen years helping leaders get more out of their strategic conversations, creating well over a hundred sessions in more than twenty industries and sectors. We've designed and led strategic conversations on a dizzying range of topics—from investment services to office furniture, from global logistics to consumer electronics, from pharmaceuticals to software, from higher education in Mexico to the future of Japan. We've led sessions in about as many subspecialties of strategy as you can think of—from corporate and business unit to innovation, marketing, technology, and talent.

Our work has taken us from formal board meetings and intimate off-site retreats to companywide jam sessions and global virtual conversations via satellite feed. We've chased bush turkeys out of a leadership-team meeting in Australia, facilitated dialogue among Catholic leaders from more than eighty countries in Rome, and helped a few thousand business leaders anticipate the global financial crisis of 2008. We've logged our ten thousand hours on this topic—and then some.

Our work, and this book, sit at the crossroads of three disciplines: strategy, design, and conversations (or group dialogue). Our purpose is not to break new ground in these established fields, which are rich with great ideas and research that we'll draw on in these pages. Rather, our laser focus is on the *intersection* between these disciplines. It's a space that has received scant attention to date but is increasingly critical to the success—and often the survival—of organizations today.

We call this space the art and science of designing strategic conversations.

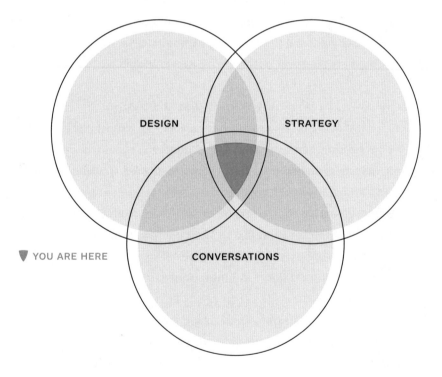

WHAT *MOMENTS OF IMPACT* WILL DELIVER

Moments of Impact is for ambitious leaders who get assigned the hardest and most vexing strategic issues in their organizations, for entrepreneurs trying to engage their boards productively, for social-change agents pioneering new business models for community impact, for hopeful educators and health-care practitioners mired in slow-to-change industries, and for enterprising business school students who have ambitions to tackle global challenges.

In writing this book, we made a serious effort to "crack the code" on what makes for effective strategic conversations. We interviewed more than a hundred people in all, including many managers, leaders, and skilled masters of this craft—a group we refer to as *black belts*. And we spent time with leading thinkers on topics that are central to strategic conversation—people such as Ronald Heifetz and Chip Conley on leadership, Peter Schwartz and Joe Fuller on strategy, Bill Moggridge and John Maeda on design, Art Kleiner and David Sibbet on group dialogue, Nancy Duarte and Dan Roam on visual thinking, Nathan Shedroff and James Gilmore on experience design, and Clay Shirky and Lisa Gansky on online conversations.

One reason it's hard to develop this skill set is the sheer lack of public examples. Most strategic conversations happen behind closed doors, rendering them invisible to all but a handful of participants. It's hard to get better at anything without seeing "what good looks like" at least a few times.

This book takes you on a power tour of some great strategic conversations. You'll see how the leaders of Hagerty Insurance reconnected with their core purpose when confronted with a choice between growth opportunities. And how the Rockefeller Foundation brought together practitioners in the emerging field of "impact investing" to turn a vague buzzword into a global network for addressing social challenges. We'll also describe strategic conversations that proved audacious in their goals and in their design—including how the software firm Intuit used a scavenger hunt to help its executives envision new possibilities in mobile platforms, and how a Catholic teaching order, the De La Salle Christian Brothers, used a customized board game to imagine a bright future despite its declining numbers.

Moments of Impact is organized to help you grasp our approach quickly and to systematically build your understanding of how it works. The next chapter ("Designing a Strategic Conversation") digs into the concept of the strategic conversation—what it is, where it came from, and why it matters—and previews the five core principles of our design process. The following five chapters share the key practices behind each of these principles, with a bit of supporting theory and ample illustrations along the way. "Confronting the 'Yabbuts'" then takes you on a short walk through the dark side of strategic conversations, helping you to prepare for the three major hurdles that often get in their way. The closing chapter ("Make *Your* Moment") ties things together and offers a few parting thoughts on how to set yourself up for success.

But that's not all. This book also features a Starter Kit crammed with tools and tips to put the book's core principles into practice—and raise the quality of your next strategic conversation.

In the age of VUCA World, the number one job of leaders must be to help organizations and society resolve adaptive challenges. It's our hope that *Moments of Impact* will better equip you to design the conversations that mean the most to the future of your organization, your career, and maybe even the world.

DESIGNING A
STRATEGIC CONVERSATION

You probably already know how to run a pretty good meeting. You know that you need clear *objectives* that are reasonable given the time you have. That you should invite *participants* who can help meet those objectives. That your *content*—presentations and reports—should lay out the issues clearly. That the *venue* should be the right size for your group and contain the necessary equipment and supplies. That your *agenda* should end with next steps, roles, and responsibilities.

This basic model works well for the vast majority of meetings: routine check-ins, formal board meetings, planning sessions, and the like. But not when it's time to have an important conversation about critical yet ambiguous issues. That's when you need a more powerful tool.

CUTTING WOOD WITH A PAINTBRUSH

We met Marcelo Cardoso in our far-flung search for black belt practitioners of strategic conversation. At the time, he was the executive vice president for organizational development and sustainability at Natura, a personal-care-products company based in Brazil. Founded in 1969 on strong principles of environmental sustainability and economic development, Natura is one of the most successful companies in South America. Today, the company generates about $3 billion in annual revenues and engages a direct sales force of more than a million women (similar to the Avon or Amway models) operating in at least ten countries across the Americas, Europe, and Australia.[1]

Part of Cardoso's role at Natura was to convene senior executives to work through the company's adaptive challenges. During our interview, Cardoso's comments about strategic conversations were insightful and nuanced. Toward the end, though, he had a confession to make. His most recent strategic conversation hadn't gone well, and he knew why.[2]

Natura's board and executive committee had come together to think about the brand values and qualities that tie together their major product lines. Brand strategy is a complex, systemic, and open-ended puzzle that cannot be resolved by analysis alone. It's a classic adaptive challenge that calls for a well-designed strategic conversation.

Reflecting on the session, Cardoso realized that he'd made two mistakes. First, the session took place in the same room where the company holds all of its standing board meetings. Second, the brand strategy conversation had been wedged into the agenda between two routine board topics.

These two choices invited participants to revert to their "default settings" for meeting interactions. The managers delivered conclusion-driven presentations instead of teeing up provocative questions for conversation, as they'd been asked to do. This approach invited board members to kick into evaluation mode and look for holes to poke in the managers' reasoning.

The session was by no means a disaster—just a missed opportunity. There was no moment of impact. "Nothing much really happened," Cardoso says. "We ended up having a regular performance review meeting instead of a strategic conversation."

Cardoso knows what it takes to run a great strategic conversation. He's done it many times. But in this instance he didn't do enough to overcome the inertia of the dominant meeting culture at Natura—and at most organizations. And he regretted it afterward.

When bringing people together, you have three main tools in your professional tool kit: a standard meeting, a brainstorming session, or a strategic conversation. Each is good for different things. The key is knowing when to reach for which tool.

It's critical to recognize early on when you are facing an adaptive challenge, call this out explicitly, and start designing your session as a strategic conversation. Then be prepared to hold your ground when the inevitable forces of inertia emerge, pushing you back toward the more comfortable—and less effective—standard meeting approach. If you don't, you're accepting a high risk that your session will yield the standard "okay" results. If you need to cut a piece of wood in half, grabbing a paintbrush is not going to work—even if it's the best that money can buy.

LESSONS FROM THE GODFATHER OF STRATEGIC CONVERSATION

Pierre Wack (pronounced *Vahk*) may be the most influential business guru of the past half century that you've (probably) never heard of. A charismatic French-German of towering intellect, Wack enjoyed the great fortune of being the right man in the right place at the right time. In another era, it's hard to imagine a student of Sufi mysticism who burned incense in his office getting much traction as an oil industry executive. But Wack's tenure as head of the legendary group planning team at Royal Dutch Shell came at a time (1971–81) when that industry, and the world around it, was changing rapidly.

The oil industry got its tickets for the rides at VUCA World before most of us. By the early 1970s, oil executives were forced to cope with a daily reality of high volatility, uncertainty, complexity, and ambiguity—in the form of unpredictable swings in the price of oil.

The price of oil matters a great deal in planning operations for an oil company. It determines how much exploration and drilling you need to do, and what costs are acceptable for developing new sources. New offshore oil rigs or cross-continental pipelines can take years to plan and execute, during which time it's possible for oil prices to rise or fall by more than half.

A faulty forecast can easily cost an oil company billions of dollars. Yet decades of experience show that nobody can reliably predict the price of oil. It turns on a wide range of external forces that no company can control: economic conditions, the cost of capital, consumer behavior, new technologies, regulatory changes, geopolitical developments, and more. During most of the 1950s and 1960s, these forces operated within a narrow enough band of variation to allow for smooth business planning. Not so in the late 1960s and 1970s.

When Pierre Wack assumed his new leadership role in 1971, Shell's top executives were already frustrated with the limitations of traditional strategic planning. They knew that the usual approach—to try to analyze their way out of uncertainty—wasn't working. But they had little idea what to replace it with.

Wack didn't know what to do either, but he was a free spirit with a willingness to experiment. He had studied the work of Herman Kahn, a brilliant US military planner who was the inspiration for the title character in *Dr. Strangelove*, the classic dark comedy by Stanley Kubrick. During the Cold War, Kahn taught military planners how to "think the unthinkable," using scenario planning and other war-gaming techniques to anticipate potential moves of the Soviet Union and other countries, with the main goal of preventing thermonuclear war.[3]

Wack embraced scenario planning—which others at Shell had already experimented with—as a supplement to traditional approaches. Instead of trying to predict the future price of oil—a fool's errand—his team created detailed, divergent scenarios about why and how the price might swing sharply up or down, which they used to test the robustness of different strategies.

While this approach made sense in theory, Wack's early attempts fell flat. He and his team would spend months researching all the key topics and analyzing and synthesizing them into clear communications packages. But their early scenario reports bounced right off Shell's managers, getting him—and them—nowhere.

During a sabbatical year in Japan, Wack spent a great deal of time studying the difference between an effective report or plan and an ineffective one. His simple but important conclusion would have a decisive impact on the future of Shell—and on strategic conversations—for decades to come.[4]

Years later, in an article for *Harvard Business Review*, Wack described his insight:

> *I have found that getting to that management "Aha!" is the real challenge. . . . It does not simply leap at you when you've presented all the alternatives, no matter how eloquent your expression or how beautifully drawn your charts. It happens when your message reaches the microcosms [mental models] of decision makers, obliges them to question their assumptions about how their business world works, and leads them to change and reorganize their inner models of reality.*[5]

In other words, Wack realized that he and his team needed to focus much less of their energy on the brilliance of their analysis and much more on the mind-set and concerns of their audience. It's rare for people to change their opinions when confronted with inconvenient facts. Rather, most humans have the agility of a Cirque du Soleil performer when it comes to twisting data to fit their existing assumptions.

The only way to change minds, Wack realized, was to build on managers' existing knowledge and experience rather than argue against it. This basic insight had a number of important implications for how he and his team worked. First, they needed to understand—and empathize with—the perspectives of managers from the inside, through deep interviewing and other techniques. Next, their presentations had to get well beyond "the facts." They needed to create stories and visuals that would resonate with managers' existing mental models and tap into the emotional and pattern-recognition parts of their brains—not just their analytic circuits.

From that point forward, Wack's scenario planning sessions always started with a "conventional wisdom" scenario—a story that best represented managers' current baseline assumptions about how the world works. Wack would treat this baseline scenario with due respect and show that many of its assumptions were valid. Then he'd gradually expand the managers' field of vision by holding up a mirror to their perspectives, turning and twisting it from multiple angles. In doing so, Wack was bending and expanding the managers' mental models one step at a time—rather than breaking or replacing them. In one article title, Wack coined a poetic term to describe his approach: "The Gentle Art of Re-perceiving."[6]

Wack and his team went on to have a legendary impact on Shell. Their work helped the company anticipate the OPEC oil embargo of 1973 and the massive disruption of oil prices in 1979, and to hedge against these huge events well in advance.[7] It gave company leaders the courage to take a strongly contrarian position; at a time when everyone else was buying tankers, Shell was unloading them. As a result, Shell leapfrogged from an also-ran among the large oil companies to an industry leader during this era. Wack and his group planning team became heroes, and Shell continues to invest in their methods to this day.

Wack is best remembered as the guy who brought scenario planning from the military to the business sector. But his true legacy runs much deeper and broader. In our view, Wack pioneered the art of strategic conversation as a discipline and practice. He was transforming the mental models of managers long before an established vocabulary or set of tools for doing so existed. His work predates the past four decades of progress in cognitive science, behavioral economics, systems dynamics, group dialogue methods, and data visualization. Lacking all this, Wack drew ideas and inspiration from where he could—Eastern philosophy, military theory, the writings of Peter Drucker—and cobbled together an approach that worked.[8]

Several of the black belt designers we interviewed told us about a time when they had a similar revelation to Wack's: an "aha" moment when they saw that their real job was not to find the right answer to an adaptive challenge but rather to help shape people's perceptions of the problem—and thus of potential solutions. Whether they realize it or not, anyone designing strategic conversations today is standing on Pierre Wack's tall shoulders.[9]

"CUTTING CUBES OUT OF FOG": TAPPING INTO THE POWER OF DESIGN

While energy was arguably the iconic industry of the 1970s, that role today is played by high technology—an industry with far more rapid cycles of strategy and planning. And if Shell was the iconic oil company of the 1970s, the iconic tech company of our time is Apple, one of the most astounding turnaround stories in business history.

Back in the mid-1990s, Apple was struggling for survival. By 2012, it had risen to become, for a time, the largest public enterprise in the world—just the eleventh company since 1925 to claim the largest market capitalization on the New York Stock Exchange. This put Apple in an elite club that includes General Electric, IBM, ExxonMobil, and a handful of other mega-giants.[10] All this with a product lineup that fits easily on the average kitchen table.

While many reasons lie behind Apple's dizzying success, design leadership is high on the list. In recent years, Steve Jobs and his colleagues have given the world an elaborate and highly profitable schooling in the power of design.

Design can feel a bit mystical, but the basics are straightforward. Design is an approach to problem-solving that strives to address user needs—often unarticulated ones—through disciplined creativity. Great design is about crafting new solutions that seamlessly integrate form and function. Solutions that, as the famous quote from Oliver Wendell Holmes goes, achieve "simplicity on the other side of complexity."

Well-designed products, services, buildings, and websites don't just look nice; they work smoothly and feel good—often in ways that you can sense intuitively but may have a hard time explaining. This effect can be found in the way Herman Miller's Aeron chair gives you firm support while allowing you room to move and breathe. It can be found in the way a Michelin-star restaurant delivers a seamless dining experience. And it can be found on Zappos online shoe store, when it serves up options uniquely tailored to your tastes. Great design delights and amazes us. It delivers solutions we didn't know we wanted—but that we "get" immediately.

Designers come to these elegant solutions by an emergent, craft-based process that follows a number of core principles—and few hard rules. These principles include:

▸ *Developing a deep understanding of—and empathy for—users and their needs.*

▸ *Cycling through periods of divergent thinking to explore diverse sources of inspiration.*

▸ *Learning through quick-and-dirty prototyping of potential solutions and adapting them in response to user and market feedback.*

▸ *Testing these solutions with a small number of users first, scaling them only after they've proved robust.*

While design is a rigorous problem-solving discipline, it can feel random at times because it often involves looping backward and trying new combinations of ideas, many of which will fail. The process appears messy not because designers are unruly but because the challenges they're trying to solve are messy. Imposing too much structure on the search for solutions would stifle creativity.

Designers are, in short, trained to navigate their way through a world of adaptive challenges. As Larry Keeley, cofounder of the innovation consultancy Doblin, is fond of saying, design is the art and science of "cutting cubes out of fog." This discipline is not just good for creating new products and services. Indeed, this may be the biggest lesson Steve Jobs taught the world: that design is equally helpful in the creation of new business models, service experiences, and entire market ecosystems.

Today, organizations of all kinds are tapping into the power of design to solve problems that reach far beyond its traditional domains. Public school systems such as the Menlo Park City School District are getting teachers to walk in the shoes of students as they rethink class schedules and overall academic and extracurricular stress load. General Electric is using design methods to turn pediatric scanning experiences into exciting jungle adventures.[11] Online creative collaboration ventures such as Kickstarter and Quirky are reinventing the way entrepreneurs get funded, design their products and services, and take them to market. Even the US Army now teaches design principles to help soldiers navigate and solve life-or-death challenges in real time as they appear through the fog of war.[12]

"Successful designers—in business or the arts—are great conjurers," writes Jeanne Liedtka, a professor at the University of Virginia Darden School of Business who has studied the convergence of strategy and design. "A capacity for creative visualization—the ability to 'conjure' an image of a future reality that does not exist today, a future so real that it appears to be real already—is central to design."[13]

In our VUCA World, organizations need to find new ways of responding to adaptive challenges. They need to get comfortable with ambiguity and seek insight from a broader range of places. They need to continuously frame and reframe not only their answers but also the questions they pose. They need, in short, to approach strategy less like mechanics and more like designers.

But talking about design, to paraphrase an old saw, is a bit like "dancing about architecture." The only way to really understand the discipline is through direct experience—ideally by doing it yourself.

THE FIVE CORE PRINCIPLES OF A WELL-DESIGNED STRATEGIC CONVERSATION

Let's return to where we started this chapter. Designing an effective strategic conversation requires that you cover all the basics of a well-organized meeting—and a good deal more. But what is "more," exactly? What does it mean to *design* a strategic conversation?

Designing a strategic conversation means creating a shared experience where the most pressing strategic issues facing an organization are openly explored, from a variety of angles. An experience where all the assumptions that make up your mental maps about how the world works—and how it is changing—are examined. An experience where new stories about your future success are explored, tested, and refined. An experience that engages a group in a deeper level of discussion than they thought possible.

The five core principles below are the main components of our process for designing strategic conversations. At first glance, they may seem like subtle refinements of the five elements of a well-organized meeting. But they're much more than that.

CORE PRINCIPLE 1
DECLARE THE OBJECTIVES ▸ DEFINE THE PURPOSE

A well-organized meeting requires that . . . you start with a clear set of objectives and desired outcomes that make sense and are realistic given the time available. These are usually expressed as a block of bullet points and shared at a meeting's outset. At the end of the session, the group can look at the list and see whether they've accomplished their goals.

A well-designed strategic conversation also *requires that . . .* you develop a clear sense of the change that this group of people needs to make together—and how this conversation will advance that process. Because adaptive challenges are rarely (if ever) "solved" within one session, you need to understand the purpose of each strategic conversation in the context of your organization's larger change efforts. At the highest level, there are just three reasons to call a strategic conversation: Building Understanding,

Shaping Choices, or Making Decisions. Any session must focus on one— and only one—of these goals.

CORE PRINCIPLE 2
IDENTIFY PARTICIPANTS ▸ ENGAGE MULTIPLE PERSPECTIVES

A well-organized meeting requires that ... you identify the most appropriate participants for a given session and prepare them well in advance. This means thinking about which leaders, decision-makers, and issue experts need to be in the room. It also means identifying any potential sticking points and "pre-wiring" these issues with participants in advance as needed.

A well-designed strategic conversation also *requires that* ... you dig deeper to understand the views, values, and concerns of each participant and stakeholder group. It requires that you find out where opinions are aligned on the key issues and where they are not. And it requires that you think hard about which *perspectives* (not just people) must be represented, such as customers or employees who won't be in the room. Ultimately, it requires that you find ways to create value from the intersection of diverse perspectives, experiences, and expertise that live inside any organization.

CORE PRINCIPLE 3
ASSEMBLE CONTENT ▸ FRAME THE ISSUES

A well-organized meeting requires that ... all content be highly relevant to the objectives and clearly communicated. Readings or handouts should be focused on creating a common understanding of the issues or posing questions for participants to think about in advance. Live presentations should deliver clear findings and present options or strong recommendations.

A well-designed strategic conversation also *requires that* ... the content and issues are *framed* in a way that illuminates different aspects of the adaptive challenge you're wrestling with, including how the various parts relate to the whole. These frames should help participants get their heads around a great deal of complexity, thereby accelerating insight and alignment. A good frame helps make insights "stick" and thus accelerates progress on tough issues.

CORE PRINCIPLE 4
FIND A VENUE ▸ SET THE SCENE

A well-organized meeting requires that . . . you find an appropriate venue given the size of your group and the nature of the meeting. Participants should be comfortable in the environment and have all the equipment, supplies, and other materials needed to support their work together.

A well-designed strategic conversation also *requires that* . . . you make thoughtful choices about all elements of the environment—from the physical space to artifacts to aesthetics. The room setup and seating arrangements should send a message about how participants are expected to relate to one another. Food and other comforts should be consistent with the tone of the session. Like a great theater production, all the parts should come together in a seamless and integrated way.

CORE PRINCIPLE 5
SET THE AGENDA ▸ MAKE IT AN EXPERIENCE

A well-organized meeting requires that . . . you follow a logical sequence of agenda items, typically starting with some form of orientation and ending with next steps. With each agenda item, it should be clear what topic(s) each item addresses and how it contributes to the objectives. By the end of the meeting, all participants should know exactly what they need to do next, and why.

A well-designed strategic conversation also *requires that* . . . you attend to the emotional and psychological experience of participants. The experience should not only be logical but also intuitive and energizing. It should tap into participants' full capabilities and perspectives—their logical *and* emotional, analytic *and* creative, selves. A great strategic conversation is not just an intellectual exercise—it's an exhilarating and memorable experience.

The table on page 33 summarizes a few of the critical differences between a well-organized meeting and a well-designed strategic conversation that we'll explain in greater detail in the coming chapters.

SOMETIMES THE RIGHT TOOL IS A COMPASS

The diagram below shows the five key elements of the standard meeting approach, represented as an archer's bull's-eye target. There's a reason why we chose this image. While most sports require a good deal of muscle memory and repetition, archery is extreme in this respect. An archer's goal is to do the exact same thing in the exact same way—over and over again. Sure, you need to consider the wind and other factors a bit when drawing back the bow. But success turns mainly on clearing your mind of distractions and faithfully repeating what's worked in the past.

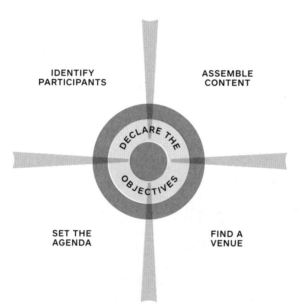

IDENTIFY
PARTICIPANTS

ASSEMBLE
CONTENT

DECLARE THE
OBJECTIVES

SET THE
AGENDA

FIND A
VENUE

**THE WELL-ORGANIZED MEETING:
HITTING THE BULL'S-EYE WHEN THE GOAL IS CLEAR**

Organizations are a lot like archers. Most of the time, an organization consists of a collection of people going through motions they've done many times before in order to produce a reliable result. Likewise, running a standard meeting can feel like aiming at a bull's-eye. Your goal is to focus all energy and resources on a pinpoint objective, such as a marketing plan or a quarterly budget. For most technical challenges, the standard meeting approach works fine.

Except when things change. Such as when your customers lose interest in what you're providing. Or when a new technology threatens to reshape your industry. At times like these, an organization can find itself aiming at a target that's moved when they weren't looking. For many, it's hard to stop doing the things that made them successful even after they no longer work.

When adaptive challenges arise and clear targets are hard to spot, you need something different to help you find your way. Something more like a compass.

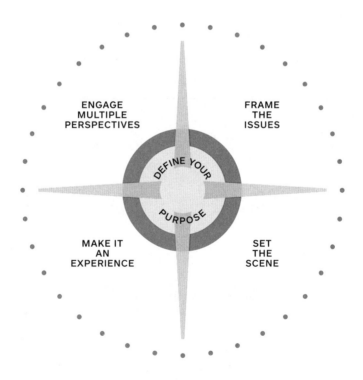

**THE WELL-DESIGNED STRATEGIC CONVERSATION:
FINDING YOUR WAY WHEN THE PATH *ISN'T* CLEAR**

With adaptive challenges, the nature of your interactions will play a huge role in determining how you resolve them. Real strategy happens in human conversations, not on lifeless spreadsheets and software. Following the five core principles in the above diagram will help you design your strategic conversations for better outcomes.

These principles can also be seen as five steps in a design process. But while we've numbered each of the core principles—and work through them in this order in the book—you don't have to complete each step and then move to the next one in a linear way. It's inevitable that you'll go back and forth among the principles as your design unfolds. The way you frame the issues might change your ideas about who needs to be in the room.

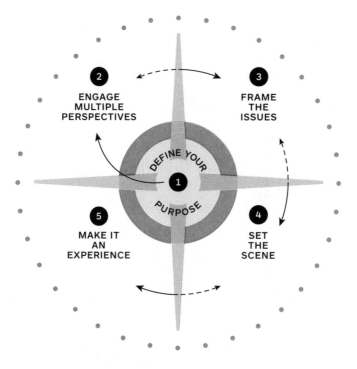

THE CORE PRINCIPLES AS DESIGN PROCESS

Thinking deeply about the experience you want to create might make you reconsider your choice of venue. Think of the five principles as a soft sequence, not a rigid one—as a set of handrails, not a straitjacket.

As you get the hang of designing strategic conversations, you'll no doubt develop refinements that work best for you. That's great. We invite you to use this process and tool kit as a platform to get on the path of mastery—and to make it your own with each new conversation.

KEY DIFFERENCES BETWEEN

A WELL-ORGANIZED MEETING	AND	A WELL-DESIGNED STRATEGIC CONVERSATION

DECLARE THE OBJECTIVES Specific objectives for the session are clearly stated (usually in bullet-point form), with an emphasis on getting to next steps	▶	**DEFINE YOUR PURPOSE** Purpose of the session is well understood, with an emphasis on advancing a larger process of change
IDENTIFY PARTICIPANTS The "right people" are in the room, with an emphasis on getting to alignment as quickly as possible	▶	**ENGAGE MULTIPLE PERSPECTIVES** The right mix of perspectives are in the room to create value by combining ideas from different places
ASSEMBLE CONTENT Relevant content is provided in a complete and well-organized way	▶	**FRAME THE ISSUES** Issues are well framed around future possibilities and key choices
FIND A VENUE Venue is appropriate for the size of group and task	▶	**SET THE SCENE** All elements of the physical environment are carefully managed to support the participants and the conversation
SET THE AGENDA Agenda is logical and in the right sequence	▶	**MAKE IT AN EXPERIENCE** Session is designed as an experience to fully engage participants emotionally and analytically

DEFINE YOUR PURPOSE

There's a great scene in the movie *Moneyball*, based on the nonfiction book by Michael Lewis. Billy Beane (played by Brad Pitt) is the general manager of the Oakland Athletics baseball team.[1] It's the 1991 offseason and the A's are coming off a good year; they won 102 games and fell just short of making the play-offs. But now they face a serious problem. Their three most valuable players have all defected to other teams for more money.

In the scene, a bunch of classic, old-school talent scouts—played by actual scouts—sit around a conference table, sharing ideas about how to replace the three stars. After listening to a rehash of options they've clearly discussed many times before, Beane loses his patience.

Beane: Guys, stop. You're talking like this is business as usual. It's not.

Grady Fuson (a scout): We're trying to solve the problem.

Beane: Not like this. You're not even looking at the problem.

Fuson: We not only have a very clear understanding of the problem we now face, but everyone in the room has faced similar problems countless times before.

Beane: Okay, stop. The problem we're trying to solve is that this is an unfair game. There are rich teams, poor teams, fifty feet of crap, and then there's us. And now we've been gutted. We're organ donors to the rich. The Red Sox took our kidneys and the Yankees took our heart.

Beane is trying to have a strategic conversation (of sorts) with his crew. But while they appear to be working on the same problem—building a winning team for next season—they're not. From Beane's perspective, the A's can't beat the rich teams by using the same talent strategy but with far fewer resources. The scouts disagree. As Fuson puts it, "This is no time to push the panic button. This is the way we've been doing it for a hundred and fifty years. Let us do our job."

The scouts see the A's problem as a technical challenge calling for tried-and-true approaches. By contrast, Beane sees it as an adaptive challenge requiring creative problem-solving. Beane is right. The only hope the A's have is to find a different approach to filling their lineup. But the problem is so familiar that the scouts are unable to think about it differently. They're trying to hit the same old bull's-eye with the same old arrow when what they really need is a compass to help them find their way.

But adaptive challenges can't be solved in one strategic conversation. In Beane's case, he undergoes a process of exploration and discovery—through a variety of activities and discussions—that leads him to a radical new strategy. Ultimately, and against heavy resistance from his scouts, he uses advanced data-mining techniques to find "hidden gem" players overlooked by other teams. He succeeds in building a winning team with a puny payroll—forever changing baseball's marketplace for talent.

KEY PRACTICE 1
SEIZE YOUR MOMENT

Imagine that your organization is facing a thorny adaptive challenge. Maybe an aggressive new competitor is stealing your market share, or an attractive but complicated growth opportunity is opening up.

Many organizations respond to the inherent messiness of adaptive challenges by trying to tame them with a highly structured process that's more in their comfort zone. But challenges like the one Billy Beane faced can't be tackled with Gantt charts and Six Sigma methods. They call for creative problem-solving similar to the kind that designers have long used to coax clarity out of ambiguity.

Once an organization recognizes that it's facing an adaptive challenge, it typically sets out on a winding road of exploration, discussion, and action that eventually leads to decisions and results. This larger process of strategic exploration and discovery can unfold over a few months or even a few years. It comprises many different interactions and touch points that unfurl over time, including informal discussions, intensive research, formal review meetings, working-team sessions, and—most important—strategic conversations.

While exploration and discovery may feel less structured than other business processes, it's no less disciplined when done well. At its simplest level, this kind of creative problem-solving follows an arc of divergence and convergence as shown in the diagram below. You start by taking a broad perspective on a challenge, then gradually shift into identifying and winnowing down possible solutions over time.

Let's say that your organization is behind the curve on social networking

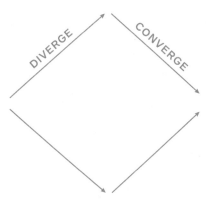

**THE DIVERGE/CONVERGE CYCLE
OF CREATIVE PROBLEM-SOLVING**

and assigns a team to figure out what to do. The team will likely start with a narrow, technical definition of the problem—such as how to develop a better presence on Facebook and Twitter. But as the team probes more deeply, they realize the issue is more complicated. What kind of communication does the organization want with its customers? How open is it willing and able to be with them? Such questions lead them to thinking about overall brand strategy, which raises the question of which market segments will be most vital to driving future growth, which . . . Well, you get the idea.

As a result, their process ends up looking more like the diagram below, with several diverge/converge cycles. The team widens and narrows their scope of inquiry at different points, with a trend toward narrowing over time. What's hard to predict is exactly when they'll need to diverge, since each cycle is driven by new insights along the way.

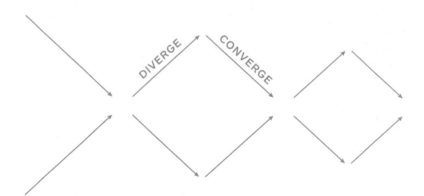

**THE DIVERGE/CONVERGE CYCLES
OF CREATIVE PROBLEM-SOLVING**

This process inevitably includes cycles of emotional highs and lows. People get excited by breakthrough insights or winning new supporters—and frustrated by dead ends, resistance from colleagues, and major surprises. There are infinite possible paths through this landscape; each situation and organization brings its own curves to this roller-coaster ride.

EMOTIONAL UPS AND DOWNS OF CREATIVE PROBLEM-SOLVING

Serious research on creativity shows that these up-and-down emotional cycles are inherent and necessary to any creative process. They can be managed but never eliminated—and you don't want to get rid of them. As on a roller coaster, the curves create a sense of energy and momentum. Novel insights rarely happen without these ups and downs.[2]

Which brings us to the role of strategic conversations. Strategic conversations are pivotal, synthesizing moments within this larger process. They enable a group to achieve new levels of clarity and coherence about their adaptive challenge—and help move leadership teams toward deeper levels of shared commitment and understanding. While an adaptive challenge rarely gets "solved" in any one conversation, a well-designed session can release tremendous energy and create forward momentum. These moments

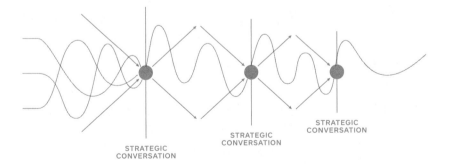

STRATEGIC CONVERSATIONS AS MOMENTS OF IMPACT

of impact propel a group forward, often opening new avenues of insight and alignment along the way.

KEY PRACTICE 2
PICK ONE PURPOSE

Ana Meade is a strategic planning manager for Toyota Financial Services (TFS)—the people who arrange financing when you buy or lease a Highlander or a Prius. An important part of her job is organizing meetings and strategic conversations. A few years ago, firm leaders felt that they were spending a lot of time in unproductive meetings. So the company launched a task force to see what could be done.

One of the improvements they came up with was a simple, one-page form for requesting time with senior leaders. At the top of the form was a big space where would-be presenters could declare the purpose of their meeting. They were required to check one—and only one—of the following boxes:

☐ *FYI*

☐ *Input (i.e., requests for guidance and feedback)*

☐ *Decision*

Straightforward, right? Not initially. "We got a lot of pushback from people who wanted to go to the executives with more than one purpose," says Meade, who helped implement the plan once it was in place. "We had to persuade people that they could really only pick one. . . . Some people also had the sense that every meeting had to have a decision involved, which isn't the case."[3]

Ultimately, this small innovation forced presenters to be clearer in their requests and helped firm leaders to know what was expected of them in each interaction. Meetings with TFS executives got a lot more focused and productive. "Just having this one question on the form has had huge impact," says Meade. "It provides clarity for everyone."

This three-part formula is almost identical to the one we've long used for strategic conversations. While there are infinite reasons to bring a group together, strategic conversations have just three overarching purposes: Building Understanding, Shaping Choices, or Making Decisions. Any strategic conversation you can imagine will sort into one of these categories. And, just as TFS found, a well-designed strategic conversation must focus on one—and only one—of these three types.

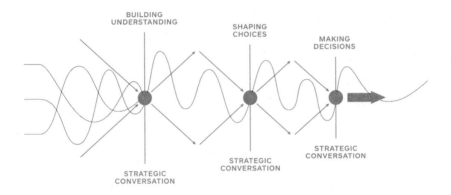

THE THREE TYPES OF STRATEGIC CONVERSATIONS

CHOOSE THE RIGHT PURPOSE FOR THE MOMENT

Because a strategic conversation consists of live interactions between people with different perspectives and passions, you can never predict exactly where it will lead. Still, you must start your design process knowing what *kind* of outcome you expect—without overspecifying the *content* of that outcome.

The first question to consider is which kind of session you need to run at this time. If your group doesn't know much about the issues—or has sharply divergent opinions on them—you need to run a Building Understanding session. If they have tons of knowledge but are spinning their wheels on what to do, it's time for a Shaping Choices session. Only when you've done both of these jobs well should you consider calling a Making Decisions session.

Most likely, some participants will—with the best of intentions—push you to mix categories of purposes in one session or press you to take the session further "downstream" than your group is ready for. *Don't do it!* Either could sink your strategic conversation. In particular, there is tremendous pressure in some organizations to treat each meeting as a Making Decisions session—even when the group isn't ready or lacks decision-making authority.

To be sure, your strategic conversation may shade a bit into the other types. A Building Understanding session might end with generating a few options to consider later. A Shaping Choices session might begin with some Building Understanding–type content or end with a nonbinding straw poll on the options in play. That's fine. But your participants should never be confused about which of the three kinds of strategic conversations they are participating in.

STRATEGIC CONVERSATIONS FOR BUILDING UNDERSTANDING: POSE A CLEAR CHALLENGE

Building Understanding is where it all starts—the foundation of any discovery process that might ultimately resolve an adaptive challenge. It's hard to get anywhere useful in Shaping Choices and Making Decisions unless you've come to some novel and relevant insights about the strategic issues that challenge your organization.

Building Understanding is hard work. Because adaptive challenges are messy and open-ended, it can be fiendishly hard to figure out how to start. It may be tempting to bring people together to explore an adaptive challenge without a clear goal in mind. Often these sessions produce a lot of great ideas, but aren't set up to accelerate real change. While such an exercise might prove great fodder for a retreat or a professional development session, it's not a strategic conversation.

While strategic conversations for Building Understanding are exploratory by nature, it's still critical to get somewhere concrete in the end. Rather than raising general issues for your group to kick around, you need to pose crisp challenges for them to wrestle with.

Imagine that you're an executive at a major book publisher, wrestling with seismic shifts in how books are produced, distributed, and bought. Your favorite bookstores are closing their doors one by one as e-books take off. Amazon, your largest and fastest-growing sales channel, has decided to compete with you by publishing its own books. Some of your bestselling authors are starting to go directly to their readers by self-publishing their works. In short, you're in the middle of a classic industry transformation marked by high uncertainty and even higher stakes.

You've been charged with convening a one-day strategic conversation for a few dozen leaders about how your markets could evolve over the next three years. While your fellow execs are plenty familiar with the issues, the high degree of noise and confusion around them makes it necessary to hold a Building Understanding session before you can think about Shaping Choices.

At first you're excited about this high-profile assignment. As the date of the session approaches, though, your anxiety soars. So many different questions and issues must be considered—and each interview you conduct or research report you read seems to surface even more of them. You've only got one day to squeeze the best thinking from all these senior people—and they're counting on *you* to make sure their time is well spent.

After working through the content, you land on four options for describing the session's purpose. Which would you choose?

▸ Option 1 (business objective focus): Meeting growth and profitability goals in a changing environment. *The world of book publishing is witnessing major changes across the entire business—from how books are acquired and produced to how they're distributed, sold, and read. In this session, we'll look at how we can meet our business goals in priority markets within an environment of increasing uncertainty and change.*

▸ Option 2 (broad trends focus): The future of book publishing. *The world of books and reading is undergoing major changes. In this session, we'll look at a range of trends that could rock the publishing world, including surprising new technologies, dramatic shifts in consumer preferences and behavior, and emerging competitors.*

▸ Option 3 (business model focus): What are the most promising new business models for book publishing? *Publishing's long-standing business model is under intense pressure, even as new media platforms are creating exciting opportunities. In this session, we'll envision some new business models that could emerge for publishing—from new entrants and established players alike.*

▸ Option 4 (reader behavior focus): How will people prefer to read in a world of unlimited choice and limited time? *Consumers are being offered more and more choices for media consumption but still face the constraints of a twenty-four-hour day. In this session, we'll take a "deep dive" into recent social and consumer trends and develop hypotheses about how reader behavior could evolve in the years to come.*

All of these sessions sound interesting. But you've got to pick one, so let's look at their pros and cons.

Option 1 asks participants to "follow the money" and focus their attention on profits and growth. It sounds tempting—but this focus is too narrow. As with Billy Beane's baseball scouts, this statement of the problem invites people to round up the usual ideas. While Option 1 offers the benefit of a strong business focus, it's unlikely to inspire much creative thinking.

With its focus on "the future of book publishing," Option 2 is the broadest. At first glance, this one sounds creative. But spending a day looking at all these trends without a clear focus is likely to result in interesting but aimless discussion, after which participants simply get back to their "real work." We've seen sessions like this lead to good results on occasion—but only when facilitated by a black belt who's great at real-time synthesis on the fly. That's a high bar to set for success.

Options 3 and 4 are much better. That's because they each pose a focused, relevant challenge that demands creative and collaborative problem-solving. Which of these options is better? Without knowing more about the specific situation, it's hard to tell. And it may not even matter. Working through either of these challenges would require the group to think about the other one as well. If you want to invent a new business model for publishing, you'll also need to understand changes in reader behaviors and preferences.

Look at options 1 and 2 again and try to imagine where you would land at the end of the day. Not easy, is it? Now look at options 3 and 4. Each provides a concrete landing point—either specific new ideas to explore or hypotheses to test. Having a clear landing point makes it much easier to conclude a session with strong insights and next steps.

For any given Building Understanding session, there's more than one "right" way to further define your purpose. The key is to pose a clear problem-solving challenge that both grounds the conversation *and* expands the group's thinking. You'll know your session was successful if participants leave with a common understanding of the issues, a set of hypotheses to test, a research agenda, or other concrete guidance for moving forward.

STRATEGIC CONVERSATIONS FOR SHAPING CHOICES: CONVERT "ISSUES" INTO CLEAR OPTIONS

Once you've built a strong platform of shared understanding, it's time to think about convening a Shaping Choices session. Action-oriented managers can only take so much talk before they start itching to do something. Converting issues into choices between specific options typically unleashes a lot of energy.

"Constructing new strategic possibilities, especially ones that are genuinely new, is the ultimate creative act in business," write Roger Martin, of the Rotman School of Management in Toronto, and A.G. Lafley, former CEO of Procter & Gamble.[4] But the way that you go about creating these possibilities makes a big difference. It's one thing to ask a group, "What should we do about social networking?" It's another to charge them with building and testing specific models for how to tap into the power of social networking in their work.

Shaping Choices follows a classic design "funnel," from generating rough ideas to prioritizing them all the way to evaluating and testing the best options. This requires making sense of a wide range of observations—from social and market trends to ground-level operational insights—and demands both rigorous analysis and creative synthesis.

Many people associate design with ideation sessions that end with lots of sticky notes scattered on the walls. But cranking out a large volume of rough ideas is just a small part of most design work—and not the most important. Far more time is spent critiquing and refining the most promising ideas. Much of the heavy lifting is done in these "crit" sessions, in which concepts are challenged vigorously from all angles.

In his book *Sketching User Experiences*, Bill Buxton, a principal researcher at Microsoft, draws a fundamental distinction between sketches and prototypes.[5] Sketches are drafts of ideas used to explore possibilities, pose questions, and provoke a response. Prototypes are more detailed models meant to describe, refine, and test potential solutions.

These design concepts also apply to strategic conversations. In the earlier stages of Shaping Choices, your group should sketch out a good number of ideas about strategic possibilities in broad strokes. In the later stages, they should build out a smaller number of prototype options in greater detail. While there may be a bit of back-and-forth between the two modes, far more time should be spent prototyping than sketching.

It's critical to have participants work at the right level of detail for where they are in the overall process. If you get too deep into the details when in sketch mode, you risk having the group reject some great ideas. If you fail to engage in sufficient detail when developing prototype options, you risk having your ideas get tripped up in execution.

When Shaping Choices, your goal is to get participants toggling back and forth between drawing a picture of an inspiring future success and testing how it could work in the real world, at increasing levels of specificity. Do this well through a few iterations and great things can happen.

SHAPING CHOICES AT TOYOTA FINANCIAL SERVICES

Remember Toyota Financial Services (TFS) and their quest for a simple formula for making meetings more productive? In 2012, TFS faced a deeper dilemma. Shifting industry and market forces were threatening the company's $7.4 billion in revenue and $1.5 billion in profits. Older consumers were holding on to their cars longer than before. A surprising number of young, urban drivers were turning to car-sharing services such as Zipcar and new on-demand taxi services such as Uber. Meanwhile, new-car buyers were demanding better loan terms, financing packages, and mobile payment systems.

TFS did not have a Building Understanding problem. They knew exactly what was happening in their marketplace. They just weren't sure what to do about it.

CEO George Borst didn't want to sit around and watch TFS's profits dwindle. "I realized we needed a motivating rally cry," says Borst. "We needed to look at every process, procedure, and product that we had. To get our profits up sustainably, we needed to turn TFS upside down and transform"—or risk getting left behind.

Borst gave Ann Bybee, TFS's vice president of strategic planning, the mandate to design a two-and-a-half-day strategic conversation for fifty-five of the company's top leaders from across business units, functions, and geographical regions. Both Borst and Bybee set the bar high. They wanted the session to be collaborative and engaging but also be grounded in present business realities—to identify cost-cutting options while inspiring disruptive new business ideas. Ultimately, the session needed to produce credible options that TFS could immediately start developing—not just a list of cool ideas. "I didn't want us to stay at the thirty-thousand-foot level," says Borst. "We needed to come up with options and leave with a clear sense of how we could take them forward."

To add structure and external perspective to their discussions, Bybee brought in Patrick van der Pijl, CEO of the consultancy Business Models Inc. and producer of the book *Business Model Generation*. Van der Pijl helps organizations shape choices, starting from a shared sense of their fundamental business model.

He opened the session by asking participants to describe the present-day TFS using the business-model canvas—a visual map with an accessible feel that highlights nine components of a sustainable business model: value propositions, customer segments, revenue, customer relationships, channels, key activities, key resources, partners, and costs (see model below). Despite a few skeptics ("We already know our business"), the conversation surfaced a surprising diversity of assumptions among participants on these important issues.

THE BUSINESS MODEL GENERATION CANVAS

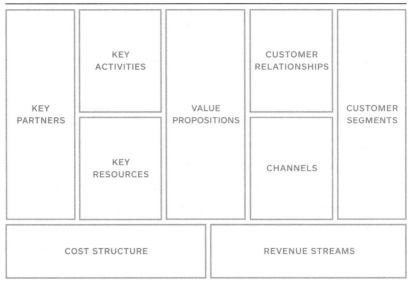

Source:
BusinessModelGeneration.com

"It was powerful for everyone to hear how many different opinions were out there on fundamental issues, such as who our customer is," recalls Julia Wada, group vice president of HR and technology. "This openness allowed us to have deeper conversations about who we were and where we wanted to go."

Two weeks before the session, Bybee and van der Pijl had asked participants to submit ideas for how TFS might take its business forward. Now, during the session, they posted about sixty of these ideas up on a board, sorted under three headings: incremental-growth opportunities, immediate cost-cutting opportunities, and bold, disruptive ideas. Participants were disappointed to see that nearly 80 percent of their ideas fit into the first two categories. At this point they were much more primed to think disruptively: What could really turn their business on its head, in a good way?

Ultimately, the group came up with four potential options for TFS to pursue. One—refining its insurance offering—was incremental. But three were revolutionary: What if TFS became the financial brand of choice for consumers? What if TFS cut its costs in half? What if TFS surprised its dealers with totally new products and services?

Working in small groups, participants mapped a detailed business model for each of these four directions. They plunged in, debating each component and sketching out their ideas. Then, rather than pass the results around the room, each group dramatized its findings, "narrating" its business model for the other participants by playing the roles of consumers, dealers, and employees in that new business. This activity transformed what could have been abstract ideas into concrete options supported by human stories of pain and gain.

After each story, van der Pijl asked participants two questions: What did you love about it? And why might it never work? The groups then recombined to explore each option in more detail. They also plotted them against TFS's existing business model and identified the assumptions and constraints underlying each possibility. What would have to be true for each strategic direction to be successful? What would TFS have to stop doing?

This method for exploring new choices was unlike anything this executive group had experienced before. "People got excited and played off one another's ideas," says Chris Ballinger, TFS's chief financial officer. "It was like there was a flywheel in the room, and everyone was giving it small kicks. They knew which direction the wheel was turning, and they wanted to get it going even faster.

"A lot of good ideas get tossed around during these off-sites, and you're not always sure they'll get picked up later," Ballinger adds. "This time we made the ideas concrete before we left and knew how we were going to take them forward. We had no shortage of volunteers who wanted to work on it in some way. I've never had that happen before."[6]

FIND (OR CREATE) A STRUCTURE FOR FLESHING OUT YOUR OPTIONS

Most participants can sense early on whether they're in a strategic conversation that's been well designed. But after a session is over, they can't always articulate why the session went so well (or not). In the case of the TFS session, at least three specific factors made it a success.

First, TFS's approach required participants to work with whole options. Too often, organizations discuss and debate half-baked ideas. Statements like "We should buy Company X" or "We should grow our business in China" may sound like full-fledged possibilities, especially if they're accompanied by reams of data. But unless such ideas have been thought through in systemic detail from all angles, they're more like idea fragments than well-developed strategic options. At the TFS session, the nine-part canvas template enabled participants to develop in a systematic way all the important aspects of the business model options they were considering.

Second, TFS's approach focused the discussion on key assumptions rather than personal positions. This point is subtle but critical. If you engage a group in conversation around the yes-or-no question of whether to buy Company X, many participants will come to a position quickly and then cherry-pick the data points that make their case. But if you have them work through *how* the acquisition of Company X *could* play out in detail— as one of several options in play—you'll often get a different response.

This approach gets participants into problem-solving rather than advocacy mode. It asks them to identify and work through the most important assumptions behind each option. Is the culture of Company X compatible with ours? If not, how does it differ and what can we do about that?

Finally, TFS's approach rendered the options in a tangible and accessible visual form—the Business Model Generation Canvas—that invited participants to engage with them actively. We'll explore this point in more detail in the chapter "Set the Scene."

The approach that TFS used is just one way to go about Shaping Choices, specific to inventing new business models. In a recent book, Roger Martin and A.G. Lafley lay out a general approach to developing and testing options. Their process is based on a set of cascading questions that can be applied to a wide range of strategic situations. Any strategic option should have a clear and interconnected set of answers to these five questions:

1. *What is our winning aspiration?*

2. *Where will we play (e.g., what customers will we serve)?*

3. *How will we win (e.g., how will we deliver a unique value proposition to the market)?*

4. *What capabilities must be in place?*

5. *What management systems are required?*[7]

Whatever process and tools you choose, it's important to find—or create—a flexible yet disciplined structure that forces participants to develop whole options; focuses the discussion on the key assumptions behind each option; and makes the options tangible. Any approach that achieves these three goals should lead to a stimulating and productive strategic conversation around Shaping Choices.

STRATEGIC CONVERSATIONS FOR MAKING DECISIONS ARE RARELY DESIGNED

This brings us to the third category of strategic conversations. As mentioned earlier, sessions for Making Decisions are rarely designed as creative and collaborative problem-solving sessions. We've only heard of a tiny number of strategic conversations that were truly designed for Making Decisions.

Why is this? The most obvious answer is that organizations are not democracies. Even the most inclusive leaders are reluctant to take a wide-open, collaborative approach to Making Decisions on their biggest strategic questions. In the majority of organizations—large or small, profit or nonprofit—pivotal choices are made by senior leaders and a handful of close confidants, not by a roomful of people in a strategic conversation.

Of course, groups of people get together to make decisions all the time—in board meetings, management-team meetings, and so on. But these sessions rarely count as genuine strategic conversations, as we define them. More often, they play out in one of two ways: the "straw poll" or the "rubber stamp." In the straw poll, a group of people who don't have decision rights are asked to weigh in on some important issues, leaving the real decisions to be made later by a smaller group. Rubber-stamp sessions are about finalizing a decision that has been "prewired" in advance among the most powerful and connected members of the group. Everyone else is effectively there to learn what's already been decided.[8]

The good news is that if you do a great job designing your strategic conversations for Building Understanding and Shaping Choices, the task of Making Decisions becomes much easier. After the first two stages, the final decision often comes as an anticlimax or fait accompli. The larger group may not have a vote, but if they've had their say in one or more well-designed strategic conversations, they've had real influence on the outcome.

KEY PRACTICE 3
GO SLOW TO GO FAST

"Creative destruction" is a central force in any dynamic modern economy. This is the evolutionary process—first described in 1942 by the political economist Joseph Schumpeter—by which innovative firms continually replace their less adaptive competitors in the marketplace.[9] Firms that want to avoid creative destruction, Schumpeter found, need to strike a keen balance between exploiting known ideas and exploring the frontiers of new knowledge—between hitting their goals for today and making wise investments for the future.

The right balance for any organization depends on the situation. Some markets—such as high tech—require more exploration than others. In our era, though, two things are certain. First, we still hire and reward people mainly for their ability to exploit known ideas (in other words, to tackle technical challenges). Second, VUCA World is serving up an increasing number of adaptive challenges, which call for more exploratory approaches—and more people who know how to lead them.

Sara Beckman is doing her part to address this imbalance. She teaches a core curriculum class, "Problem Finding, Problem Solving," at the Haas School of Business at the University of California, Berkeley. It's one of many efforts in business education today to help students develop a wider range of skills so they can tackle technical and adaptive challenges with equal competence and confidence.

In fall 2010, to better understand her audience, Beckman asked all 243 of her students to assess their own learning styles, using a well-established tool (Kolb Learning Style Inventory). What she found won't surprise anyone who works with MBAs: the majority of students fell into the Converging category—a learning style that values analysis and formal logic to arrive at quick conclusions.[10]

Dealing with adaptive challenges requires a high tolerance for ambiguity. But many leaders and managers—steeped in the Converging style of learning—are impatient with ambiguity. Change is coming at them fast, and their response time can make the difference between winning and losing in fiercely competitive markets. Also, after years of aggressive cost controls, many managers have too many responsibilities and too little time to reflect. Their daily work life is already full of things that frustrate action—such as unproductive meetings and excess bureaucracy.

Yet organizations that can't muster the patience to grapple with the volatility, uncertainty, complexity, and ambiguity of our times are ultimately no match for the powerful gales of creative destruction, which sooner or later sweep away most firms. The Oakland Athletics' scouts could execute on classic recruitment strategies all they wanted, but the rich Yankees would still destroy them unless the A's took the time to come up with a creative solution.

"AHAS" BEFORE ACTION

When approaching a strategic conversation, it's common for participants to push for agendas that drive faster toward agreement and decision-making than is realistic. That's a problem because people need time and space to process together the complexity of adaptive challenges.

In the late 1990s—a time of especially rapid change in the business world—we designed and led a Building Understanding session with a large financial services company. The emerging Internet economy was transforming Americans' investment behaviors. People who didn't know a stock from a bond before were suddenly day-trading shares in fast-rising dot-coms on the web. Huge sums of money—including the retirement funds of millions of Americans—were in play.

From their headquarters far from Silicon Valley, this company's leaders knew they needed to figure out how the Internet economy could evolve in the coming years. So the project team designed a three-day "learning journey"—a field trip to explore new ideas and environments—that included visits to about a dozen new-economy hot spots in the San Francisco Bay Area, including young but promising companies such as Google and Yahoo!

After three days of total immersion at the hub of the Internet economy, an additional day was planned for a strategic conversation.

In the weeks leading up to the event, some participants were pushing for the agenda of the strategic conversation to drive toward real action—along the lines of a Shaping Choices or Making Decisions session. However, once the group completed its intense three-day learning journey, they were overwhelmed by new information and in no position to act. They needed time together to pull out a few key insights from the learning journey before these slipped away.

During the one-day Building Understanding session, the group agreed on two important insights: that the Internet economy was real and they needed to engage with it more aggressively, and that the investment climate around the Internet economy had entered "bubble" territory, which would inevitably lead to a market correction. While perhaps obvious in retrospect, these two insights felt contradictory at the time. Getting agreement on them both was a huge win.

In the months that followed, the two big insights served as the foundation for a few more strategic conversations, which led the firm toward a number of smart decisions and actions. In particular, firm leaders resisted the powerful temptation to aggressively add capacity and staff during the heady times of 1999 and 2000. As a result, when the dot-com bubble burst in 2001, they had a less painful adjustment to make than many competitors.

This result is so important and so consistent that it bears repeating. *Before* a strategic conversation, most participants will push for session objectives that are further downstream than the group is ready for. But *during* a strategic conversation, they will push back against attempts to get to outcomes that the group isn't ready for.

As a designer of strategic conversations, it's your job to help nurture the patience that's required for the group to develop their insights *before* they start taking action. Some black belt practitioners describe this task as "creating a container for the uncertainty"; others use the phrase "go slow to go fast." Whichever phrase you prefer, protecting the space for the group to get to some real "ahas" before action is critical—and will likely test your back-bone at times. But in the end, you and your group will be glad that you did.

NEXT STEPS ARE EASY—IF YOUR GROUP IS ALIGNED

An important part of running any good meeting or strategic conversation is getting to a clear list of next steps. Time-pressed executives are emphatic on this point because they've been burned before. Like Ballinger from Toyota Financial Services, they've taken part in strategic conversations where great ideas were proposed but didn't get traction outside the room.

Poor follow-though can plague the aftermath of strategic conversations, too. Not because participants don't know how to execute, but because the group never came to alignment at all.

Pressed for time and facing a complex adaptive challenge, the default set-ting in many organizations is for leaders to push people to commit to next steps before they reach true agreement or consensus. Predictably, most peo-ple play along. Inside the room, their attitude is "salute and mute," or pas-sive acceptance. Outside the room, it shifts subtly to "this, too, shall pass," or passive resistance. There may be a long list of concrete next steps, but there's no commitment.

The psychologist Teresa Amabile found in her painstaking research of per-sonal work diaries that the single biggest factor in the morale and productiv-ity of professionals is whether they get a sense of progress from their efforts.[11] With strategic conversations, the important question is what constitutes progress. Groups that make the effort to get to a true moment of impact—that is, some deep alignment on important insights—recognize this as prog-ress. After they reach this point, they can usually start taking action—fast.

To be sure, we prefer to leave a session with both strong alignment *and* next steps. But if we had to choose one over the other, we'd choose align-ment every time. If you leave a strategic conversation without consensus, no list of next steps—no matter how "action oriented"—is likely to help. By contrast, when your group walks out of the room with genuine agreement around some important new clarity, you can always sort out next steps later.

ENGAGE MULTIPLE PERSPECTIVES

Eamonn Kelly had a problem. As head of strategy in the mid-1990s for Scottish Enterprise—Scotland's economic development agency—it was his job to prioritize and coordinate major initiatives across the agency's many units, programs, and functions. But, as in many organizations, the agency's leaders and staff were focused on delivering results within their immediate units, without giving much thought to the work their colleagues in other units were doing.

Most of the time, this close-in focus is vital to getting the job done. But myopia has its downsides. It's tough to drive the economic development of an entire country if the programs for labor-force development, export promotion, and small-business assistance are all off doing their own things.

Kelly had a classic multiple-perspectives problem. The leaders of Scottish Enterprise's various programs and functions had lots of valuable perspectives—they just weren't getting full value out of them. As a result, the agency was missing opportunities to spot key trends and patterns, as well as to combine forces on priority challenges. Going into an important strategic conversation, Kelly knew he needed to get his colleagues collaborating better. But how? Lecturing his unit leaders would surely backfire. He needed to find a way to jolt them into wanting it themselves.

So Kelly came up with an activity we've dubbed the "gives and gets game." Early in his session, he divided the forty or so participants into five teams, each representing their own unit: entrepreneurship, training, business infrastructure, existing-business development, and services. He then gave each team eight flip-chart sheets to fill in with detailed information about their collaborations with the other four units. The entrepreneurship team filled out one sheet each for the specific contributions (or "gives") it made to the other four units, and one sheet each for the benefits (or "gets") it received back. The other units did the same.

The groups scribbled furiously, making sure to capture every possible contribution. When they finished and went on break, Kelly gathered all their flip charts and organized them for a "gallery walk." The gives and the gets between the units were shown side by side now—from each unit's point of view.

When participants returned, they saw that—without exception—the lists of gives were all much longer than the gets. The side-by-side comparisons showed in stark terms that each unit believed it contributed far more to the other units than it received—a logical impossibility. Laughter erupted as participants moved from one flip chart to another, mocking one another's self-centered view of reality—something they all had in common.

Clearly, they'd been in denial about the quality of their collaborations. Through the discussions that followed, they also learned that their colleagues—even those whose roles and responsibilities were wildly different from their own—had surprising insights into the other units' challenges. Some of the most valuable strategic brainpower they needed was sitting just a few offices away—and it was there all along.[1]

DIVERSITY TRUMPS GROUPTHINK

Adaptive challenges are too complex for any one person to figure out, and too open-ended to be solved by analysis alone. They require leaps of insight that usually only come from combining ideas from different places in new ways.

Yet, too often, the default approach to collaboration amounts to a recipe for groupthink—the mortal enemy of strategic conversations. The psychologist Irving Janis documented the perils of groupthink in a book of that title more than four decades ago.[2] Groupthink is evident whenever a group of people shows excessive deference to leadership or consensus views, suppress dissenting voices, or shrink from surfacing and testing key assumptions behind important choices. The phenomenon has been implicated in helping to lead to the downfall of many organizations, more than a few ill-advised wars, and even the failure of a space shuttle (the *Challenger*, in 1986).[3]

Groupthink can be found in all kinds of organizations. It's what the Oakland Athletics' scouts demonstrated in spades in the scene from *Moneyball* when they insisted on trying to beat the Yankees with the same old tricks. It's what you usually get when you bring together the same people in a familiar place to solve problems in the same old way.

By contrast, serious studies of innovation and creativity highlight the importance of diverse perspectives in any search for novel solutions. This is true in art, science, and business—in historical times and in the present. Anywhere people are generating new ideas at a standout clip, you'll find a rich ecosystem of diverse perspectives coming together. You could find this mash-up of people and ideas in the cafés of Paris in the 1920s, in the bars and restaurants near Sand Hill Road in Silicon Valley over the past several decades, or on certain YouTube channels today.[4]

Great strategic conversations do this, too. They capture some of the magic of the coffeehouse, the scientific lab, and the after-hours bar where great cooks or musicians or entrepreneurs swap their latest ideas. To get some of this magic working for you, you have to do at least three critical things: bring together the right perspectives, create a common platform for collaboration, and carefully lean into the most important differences of opinion in a way that sets off a "controlled burn" of contained and productive conflict.

KEY PRACTICE 1
ASSEMBLE A DREAM TEAM

Getting the best possible group into the room is key to a successful strategic conversation. Yet coming up with your list of participants can be stressful—in the same way that narrowing the guest list for a wedding with a strict head-count limit can prove nerve-racking. Too often, this stress causes project teams to start compromising almost immediately. They want to come up with a "dream team." But what they end up with is a "must-invite team"—a list of people they think they have to invite, instead of the ones they need to get the job done.

This must-invite team typically includes four types of characters: sponsors, experts, doers, and vetoes. Sponsors are senior people whose support is needed to move forward. Experts are people with subject-matter expertise on the issues under discussion. Doers are people who will push the work forward. And vetoes are people with the potential to kill or undermine the project. There's a sound rationale for caring about what each of these characters thinks. They're probably a good crew for evaluating and implementing new solutions—but not for generating them.

When drawing up their participant lists, most project teams are both too inclusive and not inclusive enough. While they fill the list with people they feel obliged to include, they end up excluding—or don't even think of—other people who could be a huge help.

The choice between a dream team and a must-invite team can easily spell the difference between a successful strategic conversation and an okay one. If you want to get a dream team working on your important challenge, you need to adopt a different mind-set and set your sights higher.

MIXOLOGY 101: THE SOCIAL SCIENCE OF GREAT GROUPS

From the extensive research on creative collaboration in recent years, three findings are especially relevant to pulling together a dream team for your next strategic conversation.

First, *good ideas often come from bridging the gaps between people and groups with different areas of expertise.* In his book *Where Good Ideas Come From,* Steven Johnson coins the term *the adjacent possible* to describe the combining of elements to make something new—as in biological evolution, where new traits are far more likely to emerge from the mixing of adjacent species (such as different species of apes) than from between far-removed ones (such as a gorilla and a shark). "The history of life and human culture," Johnson writes, "can be told as the story of a gradual but relentless probing of the adjacent possible, each new innovation opening up new paths to explore."[5] This process helps explain why cities are hothouses of progress— it's easier for people and ideas to interact when they're in proximity.

It's long been known that people tend to get their jobs through "weak ties"—from a friend of a friend rather than through close friends or total strangers.[6] That's the power of adjacency. In the lingo of social network theory, however, most people live in dense "small worlds" of social connection that are separated by gaps, or "structural holes." People who can bridge these gaps create valuable connections between people and ideas.[7]

In a well-cited paper, "The Social Origins of Good Ideas," University of Chicago sociologist Ron Burt shows the value of making connections between adjacent small worlds within one organization. His research was based on a detailed survey of 673 supply-chain managers at a large electronics company. The survey asked each manager to name those colleagues he or she talked with most about ideas at work, which was used to create a detailed map of personal networks. Managers also submitted the best idea they were aware of to improve supply-chain performance at the firm. The resulting 455 ideas were then given to a panel of senior managers, who rated them on a scale of one to five for potential value to the business.

The results confirmed Burt's hypothesis: senior managers rated the ideas of the managers with broad networks much higher than those of managers whose networks were more limited (without knowing which was which). The managers who spent more time reaching across company silos had a huge advantage in coming up with new ideas.[8]

Second, *novel solutions to stubborn problems often come from outsiders and nonexperts.* The history of innovation is full of stories about outsiders who discovered breakthroughs that took experts by surprise. These outsiders might come from adjacent spaces—or from out of left field. A lowly patent clerk transformed the field of theoretical physics (Albert Einstein). A hedge fund analyst revolutionized access to high-quality education (Salman Khan of Khan Academy). Two Internet entrepreneurs without publishing experience forever changed how reference encyclopedias are created and used (Jimmy Wales and Larry Sanger of Wikipedia). Part of what made these and many other great innovators successful was that they weren't beholden to the conventional wisdom of the field in which they chose to make their mark.

That's the founding premise behind InnoCentive, an online broker that provides access to a network of thousands of experts in a wide range of fields. Its clients are mostly large companies—in pharmaceuticals, consumer products, and chemicals. Most have massive R&D budgets and deep benches of PhDs, yet they turn to InnoCentive for help in solving gnarly scientific and technical challenges. A major study of InnoCentive success stories found that, on average, physicists were more likely to find solutions to chemistry problems than chemists, and chemists were more likely to find solutions to biology problems than biologists. This counterintuitive finding confirms the power of bringing fresh perspective to vexing challenges.[9]

Third, *the most productive groups are often those with moderate levels of familiarity.* When a group works together for the first time, they can spend a lot of time figuring out how to collaborate. But if a group works together on one project after another, they can get stuck in habits and routines that aren't conducive to creative insight. A painstaking study of Broadway musical productions over several decades found that the most successful shows—in both creative and commercial terms—tend to come from teams comprising a core group of people who've worked together before plus a few fresh faces. Teams made up only of people who had worked together many times before or of first-time collaborators fared less well with critics and audiences, on average.[10]

DIVERSITY ROCKS—BUT WHICH KIND?

So you need to bring together diverse perspectives if you want novel solutions. But diversity—even within one organization—can take many forms, as the diagram below shows. You can't possibly take into account—much less optimize for—all the possible combinations of these perspectives when designing a strategic conversation. Thankfully, you don't need to. Your purpose isn't to gather a Noah's ark of token representation. It's to find creative and effective solutions to real challenges.

A DIVERSITY OF DIVERSITIES

ORGANIZATIONAL DIVERSITY
Professional role and area of expertise
Level of seniority
Organizational unit affiliation
Geographic affiliation (regional and local)
Stakeholder type

SOCIAL DIVERSITY
Gender
Age and generation
Race and ethnicity
Culture and language

PSYCHOLOGICAL DIVERSITY
Personality types
Learning styles and "intelligences"
Religious, political, and other value systems
Personal motivations and "currencies"

When designing a session, you need to ask which kinds of diversity matter most to the issues your group will be discussing:

▸ *If your challenge is about new offerings and your customers are 50 percent female—yet your invite list is 80 percent male—you need more gender diversity.*

▸ *If your challenge is recruiting talent and most of your new recruits are under thirty but most of your managers are over forty-five, you need age diversity.*

▸ *If the boundaries of your industry are blurring in ways that are disrupting your core business, you need to include people with expertise in adjacent markets.*

▸ *If your group has unsuccessfully wrestled with a challenge before, you need to infuse your conversation with fresh outsider perspectives, such as different personality types, people on the edges of your organization, or outside people with relevant expertise.*

While the above points may seem obvious, it's remarkable how often these basic adjustments aren't made. In drawing up their guest lists, many teams are reluctant to get out of their comfort zone—or push leadership out of theirs—even when that's exactly what's needed.

PUTTING TOGETHER YOUR DREAM TEAM

Given the above observations, what might a dream team for your next strategic conversation look like? Remember the imaginary case from the last chapter, where you were asked to choose the purpose for a Building Understanding session on the future of book publishing? Imagine that this session is coming up soon, and you've decided to focus on exploring new business models. Remember, your industry is going through massive change. You have to find new ways of going to market—or face near-certain long-term decline.

Your next job is to pull together a list of twenty participants. Given that most of your colleagues are experts in book publishing, you could easily fill the room with company insiders who know the business inside and out. That's what most organizations would do. But that sounds more like a must-invite team than a dream team. After the first dozen or so company insiders, each person who enters the room with similar experience won't add a ton of value.

Now, let's try building a dream team, which still begins with inside experts. Given the cross-cutting topic, you might start with a core group of ten company insiders with a range of expertise across marketing, sales, editorial, finance, and operations. Ideally, they are the sponsors, experts, and doers with the most to contribute to the topic. (Try to engage the vetoes in other ways.) Most important: make sure a critical mass is comfortable with uncertainty and open to the possibility of significant change.

How should you fill the remaining slots? We'd suggest including one or two people from each of the following categories:

▸ Voices from the frontier: *Those working at the edges of the company, such as in an experimental unit or a geography where changes are happening faster (internal to the organization).*

▸ Hubs and connectors: *Those known for building bridges between different groups (internal).*

▸ Ringers: *Those working with leading-edge technologies related to new media (could be internal or external to the organization).*

▸ Lead adopters: *Those experimenting with new media possibilities as users (internal or external).*

▸ Adjacent experts: *Those with expertise in emerging business models from markets outside traditional book publishing (internal or external).*

▸ Reader advocates: *Those representing your traditional consumer base, such as a savvy bookstore owner, well-networked distributor, or prominent book critic (external).*

Which strategic conversation do you think would produce better results: the one packed with publishing experts from inside the company or the one featuring a core group of ten company insiders plus ten of the people above? Which one has a better shot at helping the company respond to its business model challenges? Which one would *you* rather go to?

The best composition depends on the situation and session's purpose. The above group would be great for a Building Understanding session. For a Shaping Choices session, you'd want a somewhat different list—one with fewer curveball throwers and more people who will be responsible for implementing the options, to make sure they're viable. But the same principle applies: get as much of the right kinds of diversity in the room as possible to get the job done.

OPEN THE WINDOWS AND DOORS—
AND RELEASE THE HOSTAGES!

We realize that getting the dream team in the room isn't always easy. The pressure to bring together the must-invite team can get fierce. Often, you have to compromise and settle on a list that's somewhere in between. But before you cave to these pressures, it's best to think a little harder about your options.

This brings us to a simple but important observation: while perspectives come from people, those people don't always need to be physically present at your session. It's possible to include perspectives through interviews and surveys, video, audio, and the like. This has two big implications for pulling together your group.

First, it means that you have more options than you think regarding your less productive must invites. You know them: they're the ones who act like fidgety hostages, sneaking out whenever they can and tapping away on their smartphones during key points in the discussion. These people will sap energy from your session. Try offering them the option of making their points through a pre-meeting interview. Though many people want to have a voice on the big strategic issues, not everyone is itching to devote a full day (or more) to them.

Second, with a bit of creativity and flexibility, you can bring together more dream-team perspectives than you think. Even if the world's leading expert on your topic can't travel to your session, maybe she can videoconference in for an hour. Or, if you need more authentic customer perspectives, why not let customers speak for themselves instead of treating them as data points? As Kevin Blue found, even a virtual drop-in visit as short as ninety seconds can have a big impact.

Blue is associate athletic director for business strategy at Stanford University, a college-sports heavyweight and member of the NCAA's Pac-12 Conference. It takes a large budget—and a lot of fund-raising—to support Stanford's three dozen varsity teams. A couple of years ago, Blue became concerned that more than 70 percent of all contributions were coming from alumni who had graduated at least four decades ago. While an age bias is expected among donors, this percentage was greater than for the university at large and raised questions about the long-term health of Stanford's athletics fund-raising.

Blue sought support from the school's athletics board to devote more resources and energy to building relationships with younger alumni. Though he had solid data to make his case, he knew he needed to do more to drive the point home. So he grabbed a cheap video recorder and went straight to the source, conducting interviews with students and young alums, asking them just one question: "Do you know what the Buck/Cardinal Club is?" (It's the name of Stanford's club for athletics donors, which dates to 1934.)

"Many of them had no idea what it was," Blue recalls. "It's particularly striking when you talk to a scholarship athlete in the weight room, working out in a gym that's built by the Buck/Cardinal Club, on a scholarship that's funded by the Buck/Cardinal Club, and if you ask them what the Buck/Cardinal Club is, they don't know. They were giving all these humorous answers—like, 'I don't know, is it a rodeo?'"[11]

While the board was already aware of the situation, the ninety-second highlight clip brought the point to life in a way that no graph or table could. "It was a vivid and concrete way of showing this disconnect to our board," Blue says. "When they saw the videos, their mouths just flew open." As a result, the board gave Blue and his team the approval they needed to do much more aggressive outreach to younger constituents. Even though the students and young alums never walked in the room, their voices were clearly heard—and made a real difference.

KEY PRACTICE 2
CREATE A COMMON PLATFORM

Once you've got the right perspectives lined up for a session, you need to start building what black belts call a *common platform* for creative collaboration. This is an important task because strategic conversations don't always bring out our better selves. In his book *Your Brain at Work*, David Rock gives a tour of recent neuroscience research that explains why professional work can be so stressful. Several of the stressors that he cites are especially true of strategic conversations.

Strategic conversations raise uncomfortable uncertainties. The human brain is a nonstop prediction machine that's always trying to figure out what's coming next and deeply craves certainty. By definition, strategic conversations focus on uncertainties, which can make people uncomfortable and require extra neural energy to process.

Strategic conversations create status anxiety. Our evolutionary ancestors depended on social connections for survival in a hostile world. While our environment has changed a lot since then, our primal brains still perceive any threat to our social status as a threat to survival. Because strategic conversations always include an element of personal performance, they can put people's status on the line.

Strategic conversations carry real potential for loss. Strategic conversations almost inevitably create winners and losers. Depending on what choices are made, some people and parts of the organization will get to be the heroes—and others won't. Some strategic conversations even call into question the viability of the organization as a whole. (Strategic conversations also offer vast opportunities and upsides. But due to our species' well-documented bias of loss aversion, we tend to fear losses far more than we crave gains.)[12]

Strategic conversations raise the possibility of conflict. While most professionals are socialized to behave well in strategic conversations, these events can create real conflict between individuals, triggering fight-or-flight responses.

On this last point, Rock observes:

The threat response is both mentally taxing and deadly to the productivity of a person—or of an organization. Because this response uses up oxygen and glucose from the blood, they are diverted from other parts of the brain, including the working memory function, which processes new information and ideas. This impairs analytic thinking, creative insight, and problem solving; in other words, just when people most need their sophisticated mental capabilities, the brain's internal resources are taken away from them [*emphasis added*].[13]

It's no wonder strategic conversations can be physically and emotionally exhausting for participants. These sources of stress can be especially intense when the issues are important, the participants don't know one another well, or their perspectives are sharply divergent.

As a designer of strategic conversations, a critical part of your job is to find ways to offset and manage these stresses by creating a common platform to support creative collaboration. In meeting-speak, people often talk about "level-setting" a group—or making sure they start from a shared information base. While that's important, in our experience it's just one of eight key "planks" that make up a strong common platform for strategic conversation.

EIGHT KEY "PLANKS" TO A COMMON PLATFORM

1 A sense of shared purpose and objectives (covered in the last chapter).

2 A sense of group identity and community.

3 A common understanding of the challenges.

4 A sense of urgency.

5 A shared language system or common definition of key terms.

6 A shared base of information to draw upon.

7 The capacity to discuss tough issues.

8 Common frames through which to see the issues (covered in the next chapter).

While it's possible for a group to stand on a platform with five strong planks and three wobbly ones, their footing will be surer if all eight planks are solid. Does your group have a decent understanding of the challenges but lack a sense of urgency? Do they have a strong group identity but avoid tough topics? Depending on the purpose of your session and the nature of the group, you'll probably want to thump on a few of these planks with a strong hammer.

In the opening anecdote to this chapter, Eamonn Kelly used the "gives and gets game" to do a bit of platform-building before asking his group to collaborate on cross-cutting strategic initiatives at Scottish Enterprise. By our count, he was shoring up at least three planks—by helping the group see the challenge together (plank 3), raising the urgency to collaborate better (plank 4), and developing the group's capacity to discuss tough issues (plank 7).

Our colleague Andrew Blau took a different tack when leading a strategic conversation for a major arts-education institution. Most of the thirty or so participants had worked closely together for a long time—some for more than two decades. Much like the Scottish Enterprise team, they came into the conversation primarily wearing the "hat" of their department, not the organization as a whole. Plus, the strategic issues on the table had the potential to trigger anxiety and competition for scarce resources. Blau knew that at least some participants would enter the room feeling protective and defensive.

In this situation, Blau decided to strengthen the group's sense of shared purpose (plank 1). At the beginning of the program, he asked each person to describe the earliest meaningful event from his or her childhood that spoke to his or her commitment to arts education. After initial surprise at the question, people opened up. One man recalled how his mother would practice piano at night after he went to bed because it was the only time she could steal a chance to play. One woman remembered piling into a school bus full of excited kids to drive several hours to Chicago to see their first big-league theater production—a performance of The Nutcracker. Another man told the story of his grandmother's scolding him for re-creating East Los Angeles graffiti art on his bedroom wall.[14]

Even though many participants knew one another well, they had seldom—if ever—shared their personal connections to arts education. While no single question can make internal competition disappear, this icebreaker exercise helped create a strong platform for working through difficult issues that could have divided them as a group.

In a very different situation, a global transportation company was facing a tough business environment after the financial crisis of 2008. Like many companies, it had made aggressive growth investments in the years before the crisis and now had to course-correct. A consulting team started its work by interviewing thirty-plus firm leaders, expecting them to be downbeat. They found something a good bit worse: a full-on crisis of confidence at the top of the house.

With some apprehension, the consulting team delivered an initial report on the interview results at a meeting with a small group of senior executives. To their surprise, the grim report produced more yawns than fireworks. The executives found the explosive results unremarkable.

After the meeting, consulting team members reflected on this unusual reaction. By any standard, the interview results were newsworthy. The team had been planning to share them at an upcoming strategic conversation with a larger group—but they now knew they needed to do so in a more powerful way than through a slide presentation. Luckily, in the weeks that followed, the team came up with an inspired idea for sharing the results.

On the first evening of the two-day event, at an off-site retreat location, participants gathered for drinks before dinner in a spacious reception area. They'd survived an intense day of discussion, and many were exhausted. In the reception area, a surprise awaited them: an unusual installation, almost like an interactive museum exhibit, consisting of eight listening stations. As participants entered each station, drinks in hand, they were surround-sounded by dramatic readings from the inflammatory interviews. But rather than hearing their own voices, the interview highlights were read by professional actors.

The interview clips—all of which came from the very people now circulating from station to station—painted a stark picture. Yet the experience had an oddly calming effect. Because the comments were delivered by anonymous voices, they were disconnected from specific individuals. That bit of distance gave participants new perspective on the commentary they were hearing.

The next day, everyone loosened up. What had felt undiscussable the day before now felt more manageable. The group was finally ready to talk about the tough issues (plank 7). With this common platform in place, participants could get down to business.

Finally, when building a common platform, you need to consider what kind of group you're working with. Is this a group that regularly works together? Or is it a bunch of people who don't know one another?

With groups whose members know one another well, it's important to invest time in understanding the complex relationships among them that will inevitably shape their interactions. Plus, the platform that you build may remain in place well after the session is over. With more ad hoc groups, you'll usually want to construct a lighter "pop-up" platform that works for just a day or two. With groups that are a combination of the two, you'll want to think about how to build a bridge between the participants who are part of the "in" group and those who are passing through.

KEY PRACTICE 3
IGNITE A CONTROLLED BURN

Once you've got a diverse group standing on a common platform, it's time to start mixing it up. Like other forms of innovation, creating novel strategic insights and options is all about recombination. You've got to shake up the usual array of observations to get somewhere new. It's hard to get people's ideas to start scrambling without a bit of conflict and drama.

Most organizations—and most people—avoid conflict. Conversely, some organizations seem to like conflict a bit too much: in these settings, people are typically either talking or "reloading" for their next comments—with little listening going on in between. These two extremes can be equally lethal to your session, in different ways. Whereas conflict-averse groups tend to smother strategic conversations in niceness, conflict-happy groups strangle them with debate.

There's a better way to talk about challenging topics. Ronald Heifetz calls it "orchestrating the conflict."[15] We like to think of it as setting off a "controlled burn"—similar to the kind that firefighters create to protect and nurture forest ecosystems. Forests need the occasional fire to clear out deadwood and release nutrients. Under the right conditions, carefully sparked fires can help forests regenerate and reduce the chance of catastrophe. Areas without controlled burns have fewer fires—but when they happen, they're massive.

In most strategic conversations, you'll want to ignite one or more carefully controlled burns to safely start the ideas going. Below are eight different ways to get a group to talk about combustible topics while keeping a bit of distance from the heat that they throw off. An effective approach usually involves some combination of tactics, so be prepared to mix your own custom accelerant (or retardant) from these.

EIGHT TACTICS FOR IGNITING A CONTROLLED BURN

1   Take a longer time perspective on the issues.
2   Take an "outside-in" perspective, focusing on external drivers of change.
3   Turn the challenge into a game or simulation.
4   Focus the discussion on key assumptions, not conclusions.
5   Have people walk in the shoes of others.
6   Make the group grapple with tough trade-offs.
7   Agree on neutral criteria for making choices.
8   Set and maintain clear boundaries and ground rules.

When sparking a controlled burn, the first thing to consider is whether the situation calls for cranking up the heat or finding ways to contain it.

Remember Neil Grimmer, the CEO of the baby-food company Plum Organics? He saw the need to turn up the heat on the issue of competition, which his board was well aware of but hadn't addressed with enough urgency. In this situation he used a war-gaming simulation (tactic 3) that asked his board members to walk in the shoes of their competitors (tactic 5).[16]

Imagine you're a Plum Organics board member. During a meeting, Grimmer turns to you and asks, "If we're successful in hitting our growth targets this year, how do you think Gerber will respond?" As someone who follows the industry closely, you'll no doubt have some thoughts on the subject.

What if Grimmer puts the question to you differently—more like the way he set up his war-gaming exercise. This time he says, "I want you to play the role of Gerber. You're the dominant player in the baby-food business, with eight decades of history and the global power of Nestlé behind you. I'm a small niche player who's picking off some of your most profitable customers. This year, I've got plans to grow even more aggressively. What are you going to do about it?"

This is the difference between speculating intellectually about others' perspectives and getting inside their heads. Neuroscientists and psychologists use the terms *mentalization, theory of mind,* or *perspective taking* to describe the latter phenomenon (with differing connotations). Whichever term you prefer, when this shift in mind-set is activated, you can literally see it light up in brain-imaging tests.[17] By getting his board members to step inside the perspectives of their competitors in a visceral way, Grimmer turned up the heat on his strategic conversation, leading to a better result.

Sometimes, you need to turn the heat down. A few years ago, a consumer electronics company was designing a strategic conversation around a topic that was plenty flammable: how to divide up scarce budget resources in a time of major change.

After riding a long period of gradual market transition, company leaders faced two massive shifts at the same time. Consumers were rapidly moving their digital lives from PCs to tablets and mobile phones. Meanwhile, online social media—after being hyped for years—were now competing in earnest with traditional advertising channels for attention and money. These shifts posed a serious threat to both the products and the marketing strategies that had made the company successful.

The situation was especially acute for the chief marketing officer (CMO), who controlled a large budget that offered the company's best hope for protecting market share in the current year. He and his team were struggling with questions about how quickly to move marketing resources from PC-based products toward other platforms, and from more traditional marketing channels (such as TV and print ads) toward social media campaigns on Facebook and Twitter.

The typical annual budgeting process is routine and yet also shrouded in mystery for most people. Different units and functions prepare their requests for the coming year (which sometimes read like wish lists to Santa) and send them up the line. This "roll up" of unit requests almost always exceeds the total budget available, sometimes by a lot—setting the stage for intense backstage lobbying. The budget is then decided and announced, but the rationale often remains opaque.

This "black box" budgeting process works well enough most of the time. But not when an adaptive challenge rears its head. Given the rapidly shifting market dynamics, the CMO knew he needed to tap into the best thinking from the company's top marketers. Rather than round up the usual wish lists, he decided to bring the four teams together to wrestle with the tough budget trade-offs in a live strategic conversation. This solid idea was also daring. Unless well handled, the approach could spark a fierce political bonfire.

In the weeks leading up to the session, the CMO's team set about creating the right conditions for a controlled burn. They spent time with each of the marketing teams, listening to their issues and reviewing their initial budget requests. They also worked with the four teams to develop a set of criteria for decision-making, which would be neutral enough for all divisions to support.

In the strategic conversation, thirty people—mainly marketing leaders from corporate and the four divisions—worked together for one day. The group spent most of the morning immersing themselves in the global trends that were driving change in their markets. These discussions made clear that the company's status quo budget was not an option and created a strong common platform.

In the afternoon, the project team divided participants into four groups, each with a mix of representatives from the four divisions. Each group was given the same set of companywide goals and criteria, a large matrix for allocating resources across different products and channels, and just a few hours to come up with a new marketing budget for the entire firm.

In this way, the four groups were each carefully lowered into a controlled blaze defined by clear boundaries. Their goal was not to resolve the budget in one day—ultimately, that decision still rested with the CMO. Rather, the goal was to ensure that a wide range of ideas would surface and recombine, igniting new ideas. In effect, the team's design combined four of our eight tactics: it focused on the external drivers of change (tactic 2); forced participants to grapple with trade-offs (tactic 6); used neutral selection criteria (tactic 7); and set clear boundaries and ground rules (tactic 8).

The four groups produced draft budgets that were more realistic than the requests made prior to the session—and were much more aligned than expected. From this running start, the CMO was able to produce a final budget (in just a few weeks) that was responsive to market conditions and enjoyed broad support across the divisions.

When you approach a strategic conversation, some of the most important choices you'll need to make are where, when, and how to light a fire to get breakthrough insights. To get there, ask yourself these questions:

▸ *What differences can you lean into that will incite a bit of conflict and drama?*

▸ *Is your challenge finding a way to crank up the heat—or finding a way to contain it?*

▸ *Which combination of the eight tactics could be most effective in your situation?*

THE AMAZING POWER OF LISTENING LIKE YOU GIVE A DAMN

To solve big adaptive challenges, you've got to engage multiple perspectives. The good news is that most organizations are full of diverse perspectives. The less good news is that they all create their own version of the silo problem. It's human nature that we build boundaries around ourselves as individuals and as groups for protection. That's never going to change. What's more, jawboning people to play nicely together rarely works. At best, you'll get their compliance for a few hours—not their full engagement.

In this chapter, we've laid out a few key practices for engaging multiple perspectives effectively. These practices can unleash a ton of value by lowering silo walls—even if they never disappear. But by themselves, these are still not quite enough. Not without one secret ingredient known to all strategic conversation black belts.

They listen—a lot. In almost all the successful strategic conversations shared in this book, the project team conducted pre-session interviews with most or all of their participants. During these interviews, they didn't do the let's-borrow-your-watch-to-tell-you-what-time-it-is kind of listening. They actively listened, then stewed in the interviews afterward to find the hidden patterns within.

When you listen to people talk about their toughest challenges, several important things happen. You begin to see many different sides of the issues. You develop sympathy—and empathy—for people's various perspectives, even those that contain flaws. And you start to see the underlying dynamics of an issue, including the deep grooves of conflict and congruence. When you've listened well—and with a bit of distance—you'll see these patterns better than the people who are immersed in them.

To be sure, your understanding can never be perfect. People will hold back on some sensitive topics, and you'll bring your own biases as well. But if you can begin to internalize the full range of perspectives in play, your ability to engage multiple perspectives can shift by an order of magnitude.

When you listen deeply to participants, you'll make design choices that reflect their perspectives and resonate with them. When participants enter your session, each person will feel heard, even if he or she doesn't agree with all of your choices. When people feel heard, their stress levels fall. When people are less stressed, they're more open to listening to others. By developing and showing genuine empathy, you're more likely to create an environment in which participants show empathy toward one another.

On occasion, we've had to run sessions without being able to do interviews in advance, and the results are never as good. A black belt practitioner can still design and run a strategic conversation that's professional and well put together. But the result will be a somewhat awkward fit, like the difference between a suit that's off the rack versus one that's been custom-tailored. The off-the-rack suit may be well made—but it wasn't made *for you*.

If you take the time and effort to listen deeply to people up front, the rest of this process becomes much easier. You'll do a better and more efficient job of framing the issues, setting the scene, and creating an overall experience that resonates with your group—topics that we'll cover in the coming chapters. In short, you'll seriously raise your odds of creating a moment of impact.

FRAME THE ISSUES

Have you ever seen the invisible gorilla? A few years ago, Harvard psychologist Daniel Simons had a group of graduate students create a rough, one-minute video clip that would soon become famous. In it, two groups of three players pass a basketball among themselves. One trio wears white shirts; the other wears black. Viewers are told to count the number of passes that the white team makes—and to ignore the black team's passes. To make things trickier, the two teams are moving around in a circle, so you need to pay careful attention.

About halfway through the clip, a woman dressed in a black gorilla costume walks right into the circle of players, pounds on her chest, and then walks away. After the clip is over, the audience response is as consistent as it is jaw-dropping. When asked if they noticed anything unusual, *at least half* the viewers can't think of anything. They never noticed the gorilla right in the middle of the screen. They're stunned when they see it on replay. How can that be?

The technical term for this phenomenon is *inattentional blindness*, which Simons and coauthor Christopher Chabris describe at length in their book *The Invisible Gorilla*. In plain terms, inattentional blindness means that we tend to see what we're looking for. The invisible-gorilla video teaches an important lesson for strategic conversations: that it's easy to miss huge things right in our face if our attention is focused just a few feet away.[1]

THE PICTURE ON THE PUZZLE BOX

Strategic conversations require participants to take in a great deal of information and observations from a variety of sources and perspectives, all at the same time. But to make progress on adaptive challenges, you as the strategic conversation designer need to do more than just gather all the relevant data for them. You need to make smart choices about where and how to direct their attention within this mass of complex and often conflicting signals.

As the word suggests, a *frame* is a strong focusing device—a set of operating instructions for the mind. The gorilla video's counting assignment is a frame because it dictates what elements of the picture your mind focuses on—or doesn't. Unlike that assignment, good frames for strategic conversation turn your attention to what matters most while lighting up your peripheral vision at the same time.

Having a strategic conversation without a strong frame or two is like trying to do a jigsaw puzzle without the picture on the box. It's possible—but damn hard. If you've ever been part of a strategic conversation that floundered, odds are that poor framing was one culprit. Bad frames can blind you to important signs of change—or even chest-thumping gorillas—that are right in front of your nose.

As a strategic conversation designer, an important part of your job is to frame (and reframe) the issues in a way that directs the attention of your group in productive ways. Black belts use frames the way photographers use lenses. They pull them out when they need to shift the focus of a strategic conversation, or to give it a different hue. If your group has tunnel vision on a problem, then you need a broadening frame or two. If they're overwhelmed with data and complexity, you need a frame that narrows. If they see only risks ahead of them, you'll need a frame that helps to highlight opportunities as well.

When practical, it's best to identify your key frames well in advance of your session. This will help you make clearer and smarter choices about which content to include—and, just as important, what to leave out.

Framing is tricky, though. Most black belts who are great at framing learned to do it by feel, through trial and error. Still, they follow a few key practices that can help you enable your group to arrive at shared insights more quickly and effectively. In particular, they develop frames that stretch—without opposing—participants' existing perspectives; they

---

FOUR FRAMING PITFALLS

Poor framing dooms many strategic conversations. Be careful not to step into these pitfalls:

- *Lack of framing or overly broad framing.* This is probably the most common mistake. In many standard meetings, the content isn't framed at all. A topic is "teed up" and people give a series of disconnected presentations on different aspects of it. The group is left to sort out which observations matter the most and to connect the dots somehow, with little guidance.

- *Overly familiar or narrow framing.* Familiar issues, framed in familiar ways, lead back to the same old ideas. Too often, the competitive landscape is framed in terms of traditional head-to-head competitors only; customers are framed in terms of current market segments; growth options are framed in terms of today's business units and divisions. Same old frames, same old results.

- *Too many frames.* Consultants are highly susceptible to a condition known in the business as Frameworkpalooza. It's named after the concert festival Lollapalooza, which features a list of bands longer than you can possibly see in one visit. Making your participants peer through lots of frames in one strategic conversation is sure to create mental whiplash and confusion.

- *Biased or overly proscriptive framing.* This mistake is less common, but deadly when it occurs. Sometimes, leaders are only interested in validating the strategic choices they've already made, so they frame issues and choices in a way that stacks the deck in favor of these outcomes. Biased frames send a clear signal to participants that they're in a "fake participation" session—an invitation to tune out the proceedings.

create opportunities for participants to think inside different boxes; and they focus their efforts on a few frames that can have the greatest impact. Because the first two of these practices are well covered in other parts of this book, the bulk of this chapter focuses on the last one: how to think about choosing a few frames that will define your next session.

KEY PRACTICE 1
STRETCH (DON'T BREAK) MIND-SETS

Anyone who's been immersed in a topic for a while inevitably falls under the spell of the "curse of knowledge": as you become more informed, you forget what it's like to not know what you know. As you prepare for a strategic conversation, this curse can kick in with a vengeance. It makes it harder to put yourself in participants' shoes—and easy to fall into the trap of organizing your session in ways that make sense to you, but not necessarily to others.[2]

Fortunately, the curse of knowledge can be overcome—but only if you make the time and effort first to understand your audience.

Remember Pierre Wack? His first attempts to engage Shell's managers in scenario planning failed abysmally. Although his team did brilliant research, the way they framed their stories about the future business environment didn't resonate. Wack's big "aha" was to start each project by understanding managers' assumptions about the future, then to build out alternative scenarios from this foundation. When Wack started framing his scenarios in relation to managers' existing mental models, he got much better results.

Wack's critical insight was that people are much more receptive to new ideas that expand on their current mental models, rather than stand in opposition to them. Your participants will surely bring their own frames—often implicit, unstated ones—with them to your session. If you don't identify and reckon with these silent frames in advance, your carefully crafted frames will end up battling with them in the room.

When creating any frame for a strategic conversation, you need to keep one eye on the content and one eye on the perspectives of your participants. When possible, this means doing what Wack's team did: working hard to understand these perspectives before developing alternative frames. It also means testing your frames with a few key people ahead of time, to make sure they resonate. When you create frames that stretch—not oppose—participants' mind-sets, they have a good chance of becoming "sticky," laying a strong foundation for strategic conversation.

KEY PRACTICE 2
THINK INSIDE *DIFFERENT* BOXES

Groups facing adaptive challenges are often exhorted to "think outside the box"—an overused cliché that doesn't provide instructive guidance.[3] To get to creative solutions, you need to help your group approach their familiar challenges from a number of angles and lenses. In other words, you need to help them think inside boxes that are different from the ones they're used to.[4]

There are many ways to do this, which we touch on throughout this book. War gaming—such as Neil Grimmer's Baby Food Fight—is one. Other options include scenario planning, simulations, and role-playing activities, such as taking on the personas of specific customers to find and solve problems from their point of view.

Here's one approach that we've seen work well. Imagine that you're designing a strategic conversation for leaders of a clothing retail chain that's steadily losing business to both online and boutique stores. You want to help them generate creative options but are afraid they'll come up with the same ideas that they always do. One way to spark their imaginations is to redesign their logo in the style of other familiar brands such as Google, Apple, and Starbucks. Then ask them to come up with ideas from inside these "boxes."

Gimmicky as it may sound, something about seeing your company's name lit up in the playful colors of the Google logo jogs the imagination. What *would* Google do to get through your nastiest strategic challenge?

Probably not the same things you've been trying. When people think inside different boxes, they almost always come up with better ideas than they would by thinking inside the same old boxes—or by thinking without any constraints, which may sound like fun but is almost impossible to do.

KEY PRACTICE 3
CHOOSE A FEW KEY FRAMES

Most strategic conversations are built around a small number of key frames, usually three or fewer. Asking a group to work with more frames is sure to create headaches and confusion (classic Frameworkpalooza). In choosing these frames, your main goals are to focus attention in the right places and to ensure that group members are solving the same puzzle together at the same time.

Frames can take many forms, including questions, catchphrases and metaphors, visual frameworks, and stories. Some forms are used more often for specific purposes: questions typically either broaden or narrow participants' perspectives, while visual frameworks help them see the full contours of an issue. We'll spend most of the rest of this chapter looking at these different forms.

FRAMING THE FOCAL QUESTION

If you had a life-threatening cancer and were offered an operation with a 90 percent chance of curing the disease, would you take it? What if you were told that there was a one-in-ten chance you wouldn't survive for long after the procedure?

These questions ask the same thing, but they are *framed* differently. People are far more likely to respond positively to the first version of the question, which highlights the opportunity, than to the second, which highlights the risk. Pollsters have known for ages that the way that you frame a question can have major impact on the answers you get. This observation also applies to strategic conversations, where a well-framed question can be one of your most powerful tools. As Charles Kettering, the American inventor and industrial engineer, famously said, "A problem well stated is a problem half-solved."

The Nueva School is a nationally recognized independent school in Northern California that until recently served only prekindergarten through eighth-grade students. Founded in 1967, Nueva is known for its progressive curriculum focused on creative learning, group collaboration, innovation, and social and emotional development. But each year, as a new class of students approached graduation from eighth grade, a significant number of students and parents felt they were leaving the unique environment of Nueva too soon and expressed their desire for the school to expand into high school.

In 2010, Diane Rosenberg, Nueva's head of school, created a special task force comprising parents, board trustees, teachers, volunteers, and subject-area experts to explore the possibility. The team of more than thirty volunteers spent months holding brainstorming sessions, interviewing education experts, researching current statistics on high school performance, and visiting more than fifty other schools across the country to better understand the ideal characteristics of their potential high school program.

One pivotal moment was a strategic conversation held on Nueva's campus with university presidents, college deans, and educational visionaries. This Presidents' Roundtable was meant to provide ideas on what high school kids needed to learn from the perspective of the institutions they would be entering.

In approaching this conversation, session organizers considered two possible focal questions: (1) *Could* Nueva build the school? or (2) *Should* Nueva build the school?

That simple word choice changed the entire nature of the conversation. A session framed by the focal question of whether Nueva *could* build a high school would invite a conversation about the viability of the plan, the amount of money it might take, the staffing and facility requirements, and so on. A session framed by the question of whether Nueva *should* build the school would focus instead on whether a new kind of high school was needed.

Eventually, the board knew it would need to address both questions. But for this session, they chose the *should* question. By doing so, they framed the strategic conversation to explore broader trends such as: What are the social issues impacting kids? How are technology trends changing the way they learn and engage with others? How can education best prepare students for an increasingly global world? And given these trends, what was missing from existing high school curricula that might better prepare kids for college and meaningful work?

In probing these questions, university leaders revealed deep concerns about the increasing levels of stress, depression, and psychological disorders among incoming college freshman. Students were arriving on university campuses with much more impressive experiences and performance results than in previous generations, but their overcredentialed applications often masked emotional or social immaturity. The leaders questioned whether high school standards needed to shift to include emotional development as well as academic rigor.

During their candid discussion, these education leaders made a compelling case for a new kind of high school that would emphasize cross-disciplinary twenty-first-century innovation skills, emotional resilience, and persistence alongside the traditional liberal arts and science curriculum. This strategic conversation—defined by its framing question and informed by four years of deep research—helped Nueva leaders and the local community see that the time was ripe to create a different kind of high school that would enable the development of well-rounded, lifelong learners who would be valued by top colleges. The new high school opened its doors to its first class of ninth-grade students in August 2013.[5]

When designing a strategic conversation, deciding what problem you're trying to solve is one of the most important choices you'll make—and one worth spending a good deal of time to get right. While there's no right or wrong way to go about this, it's usually helpful to draft three or four candidate focal questions that would steer the conversation in slightly different directions (similar to the different problem statements on the future-of-publishing example in the chapter "Define Your Purpose"). Then you can test these options with a few key people to see which one sparks the most productive reactions.

Resist the temptation to compromise by merging the questions into one high-level, all-inclusive discussion. By making a clear choice between *could* and *should*, Nueva's leaders got a clear and strong result from their Presidents' Roundtable. If they had tried to tackle both questions with limited time, it's doubtful the session would have been as productive.

A FRAME OF FEW WORDS: CATCHPHRASES AND METAPHORS

What do the following imagined quotes from a strategic conversation have in common?

▸ *"Our competitor's new offering is creating a real* innovator's dilemma *for us."*

▸ *"The only way to get decent margins is to find a* blue ocean *opportunity where the competitive field isn't already crowded."*

▸ *"If we can get our message out to enough* connectors and mavens *in the first weeks after launch, we could reach a* tipping point.*"*

▸ *"After launch, we need to take a* balanced scorecard *approach to evaluating progress."* [6]

Each of these quotes features a popular idea—or meme—touted in the business literature. At most strategic conversations, you'll hear several such memes. Sometimes they're tossed out as meaningless buzzwords and come and go like the passing of the tides. At other times, a meme can become a framing concept, a catchphrase that acts as shorthand for a more complicated idea or argument. As with the above list, the stickiest catchphrases tend to feature vivid metaphors. While you can find many framing concepts in business books, the best ones are often handcrafted.

A few years ago, the senior executive team of a large Internet-service provider wanted to enter a market still in its early stages: Internet-based video over TV. At the time, only a tiny fraction of US households were able to stream online content from their computers to their televisions. While it seemed obvious that Internet video over TV would become huge one day, when exactly the market would ripen was an open question. Entering this market ahead of competitors could prove hugely profitable. But getting in too early—at the "bleeding edge"—could be costly.

The executives had another problem: it was hard to talk about their options without getting lost in the complexity of all the related issues. After a good deal of research, the team came up with a simple frame to help company leaders think about their timing. They called it "the Drip and the Avalanche."

The Drip referred to a dynamic that had been playing out in the newspaper business for well over a decade. Since the late 1990s, newspapers had seen their readership and advertising revenues gradually drip away, as people took their news and information from an increasingly wide range of sources. However, by the time of this strategic conversation, there had been no major breakthrough in how news providers made money. The newspaper business was still essentially the same, just less attractive with each passing year, as the Drip took its relentless toll.

By contrast, the Avalanche represented a dynamic that had been playing out in the music industry. In the mid-2000s—after a long period of Drip due to Napster and other online sources—the music industry experienced a massive shift. Apple revolutionized the business model for music by enabling consumers to buy and download music by the song on its iTunes service, which they did in droves. In doing so, Apple—a consumer electronics company—rewrote the rules of the music industry, creating winners and losers in its wake. The music industry looked very different before and after the Avalanche.

At the time, the market for video entertainment still closely followed the Drip dynamic. People's eyeballs were slowly wandering away from traditional TV-based entertainment in favor of YouTube, Hulu, Vimeo, and other online sources—while the dominant business model of cable TV was still holding strong. Meanwhile, it seemed inevitable that the video market would eventually have its own Avalanche, allowing consumers to pay for what they wanted to watch, instead of monthly subscriptions for dozens of channels they didn't want.

The big question was when—and how—the Avalanche would come. The timing would, at least in part, turn on how fast customers "dripped" away from traditional sources. Eventually, the Drip would surely trigger the Avalanche—but when?

In their strategic conversation, the executive team embraced the frame of the Drip and the Avalanche as a critical shorthand device—one they continued to use well after the session was over. With each new piece of information—a new technology development, competitor move, or consumer trend—they asked themselves, "Will this help make the Avalanche come faster or slower?" These two simple words helped them process a complex stream of information faster, make smarter strategic choices, and communicate those choices clearly to others.

VISUAL FRAMEWORKS: MAPPING THE LANDSCAPE

A simple visual image is one of the best ways to help a group see the same thing at the same time. Many of the most influential ideas in the field of strategy have been expressed in memorable visual frameworks, such as BCG's Growth-Share Matrix from the late 1960s (with its cash cows, stars, dogs, and question marks); Michael Porter's Five Forces from the late 1970s (with its competitors, customers, suppliers, new entrants, and substitutes); and McKinsey's Three Horizons model from the late 1990s (with its core, grow, and explore horizons).

Visual frameworks can either be general (such as those above) or customized to context. While general frames can remain valid for a long time— sometimes even decades—most customized frames lose their relevance within a few years because they were created to address a challenge at a particular moment. Still, custom visual frameworks can make a big impact even if they're only used in one session.

A few years ago, executives at a company that makes medical devices were trying to figure out how much to invest in a remote monitoring system they had created to track data from their products. They spent a lot of time studying how other device makers in their market were investing in similar systems, and a lot of time contemplating the features and cost of their offering compared to those others.

This close-in focus on the every move of your head-to-head competitors is common to many organizations. But these days, competition can come from unexpected places, such as your biggest distribution partners (think Amazon's entry into book publishing); new entrants you didn't imagine (Airbnb's unexpected expansion of the hospitality market); or unusual partnerships (Nike's link with Apple to create the popular Nike+ platform for runners to track and share their personal performance data).

Given this reality, it often helps to expand the frame of competition to include adjacent markets and industries. In this case, to broaden its thinking, the company designed a strategic conversation on competition that resembled a two-act play. In the first act, its organizers asked participants to

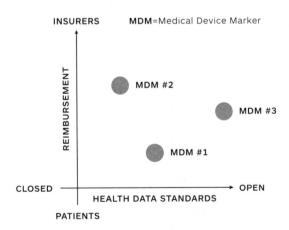

THE COMPETITIVE LANDSCAPE FOR MEDICAL DEVICE MONITORING

look at the company's market positioning choices against the familiar competitive landscape of other device makers. The executive team discussed the competitive dynamics across this visual map for a while, making similar observations to those they'd made in the past.

Then the team revealed a visual that reframed the competitive landscape to include a much broader set of competitors for health-care data management. This new map was drawn to scale, so that the familiar landscape of device makers appeared as a small fragment in the corner of a much larger playing field, which was now dominated by giants such as Siemens, Oracle, and IBM. Zooming out the frame to show the bigger picture made it sud-

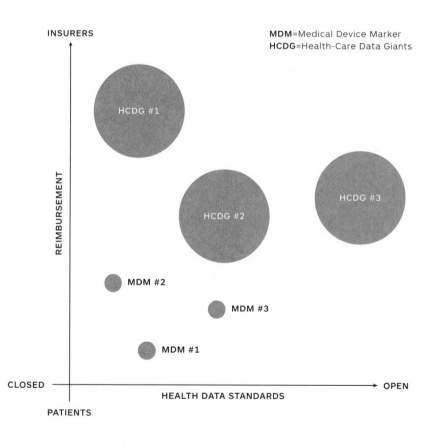

THE COMPETITIVE LANDSCAPE FOR HEALTH-CARE DATA

denly obvious that tracking data from medical devices would eventually become a feature in more comprehensive systems—not the smaller systems that most device makers were designing.

It's not always easy to point out the obvious so that people will see it. In this case, the skillful shift in frames helped move the group's focus from how to "win" in today's markets to how to best position themselves for a very different future than they'd been planning for.

Visual frames are just one form of visual thinking that can enrich strategic conversations—and a topic we'll return to in the next chapter. And they're even more powerful when used in combination with other smart design choices. Just ask the folks at Hagerty.

FRAMING THE FUTURE AT HAGERTY INSURANCE

Hagerty Insurance is the largest private employer in Traverse City, a gem of a small town in Northwest Michigan that is a regional tourist destination popular for its water sports, wineries, and boutique shopping. Hagerty is not your average local insurance agency, though. It's the world's leading agency in a highly specialized niche: coverage for collectible boats and cars.

Husband-and-wife team Frank and Louise Hagerty founded the company in 1983, mainly out of frustration. Avid collectors of classic boats, they found they couldn't buy insurance coverage for their prized vessels. They weren't alone. When they placed their first ad in a hobbyist magazine, their answering machine overflowed with calls. In 1991, Hagerty expanded into coverage for classic cars—another personal interest, and a much larger market. By 2012, the company had grown to about 450 employees.

Hagerty's growth had been due to many factors, including strong marketing and PR, a focus on customer service, and a niche market position that big insurance companies largely ignore. Perhaps most important was the company's genuine passion for collecting, which is shared by most employees today.

In 2008, with financial markets booming, Hagerty's leaders were tempted to expand their footprint in insurance—perhaps by getting into coverage for other collectibles, such as guns, sports memorabilia, or art. Considering their options, they faced a classic strategic choice: after more than a decade of strong growth, they could either double down on what had made them successful to date (and possibly face slower future growth) or move into adjacent markets (and possibly dilute their success formula).

Co-CEOs Kim Hagerty and McKeel Hagerty (daughter and son of the founders) decided to convene the top eighteen leaders of the firm to revisit its strategic direction. For this strategic conversation they chose a scenario-planning exercise focused on what the business could become over the next twelve years, to the year 2020.

Scenario planning is basically a future-simulation exercise. It asks a group to imagine operating within several different yet plausible future environments, and to experiment with possible strategic directions within each. This exercise builds on three core principles: looking at a challenge from a longer time perspective; engaging multiple perspectives; and thinking "from the outside in"—focusing more attention on how the world and your markets are changing and less on your own organization.

In February 2008, Hagerty's leadership gathered for three days at the Ritz-Carlton in Chicago. On the first day, they explored a large number of driving forces that could shape their future business environment. They looked at whether the economy would be strong or weak. They considered whether oil prices might rise or fall. They imagined how generational shifts and globalization could shape the hobby of collecting. To enrich the discussion, Hagerty had invited five external guests who brought special expertise and an unbiased perspective on these topics.

The group then entered the toughest part of the process: agreeing on a single visual frame. The group was charged with finding a two-by-two matrix based on the two most "critical uncertainties" from the long list of driving forces they'd reviewed. While there's no such thing as a "right" scenario matrix, some are better than others. Their choice would have a big impact on the strategic conversation that followed.

Getting a diverse group of more than twenty people to agree on one scenario matrix can be a high-wire act. The Hagerty group struggled mightily with their frame. They weren't sure how much emphasis to give macro forces (such as the economy or oil prices) as opposed to industry forces (such as consolidation in insurance markets) or consumer-demand forces (such as generational change or new tastes in collecting).

In the afternoon of day one, the group split into four small groups to experiment with different candidate scenario matrices. Then, each group shared the one frame that worked best for them, based on agreed-upon criteria. With four candidate matrices, the combined groups had no clear sense of which one to select and carry forward. They went out for a nice dinner and slept on the question. (An important step in any creative process.)

Day two began with open-ended reflections on the prior day's work, with the external guests playing a critical role. They had listened to Hagerty's leaders talk about the company's future from a range of angles. The guests had seen the Hagerty team "try on" different possible future strategies like so many outfits. Like an honest friend who goes shopping with you, these guests had developed a sense of which clothes seemed to "fit" the culture and values of the Hagerty team—and which ones didn't work.

The experts pointed out that the group's discussions were most energetic when they were trying to figure out how to better serve collectors—and far less convincing when they were trying to expand their presence into adjacent insurance markets.

For Eric Okerstrom, Hagerty's vice president of strategic management, a key moment came when one of these experts, Mark Miller, then editor of *Crain's Chicago Business*, observed, "You guys don't talk like *any* insurance company I've ever seen, anywhere. Nobody's talking about 'peace of mind' and risk. You're all talking about the collectors and their hobby."

In this way, the guests helped the group take a step back and see their own conversation clearly. "I'm honestly not sure we would have had a breakthrough if not for the external participants," recalls Jonathan Star, the consultant who led the conversation. "They were able to hold up a mirror on the conversation and challenge Hagerty's leaders in a way that was both credible and constructive."

The Hagerty team accepted the candid feedback of their guests and quickly agreed on a brand-new scenario matrix. This visual frame was based on two critical uncertainties: (1) the extent to which collecting in the future would be an individual or a community pursuit; and (2) the extent to which collectors would focus on tangible items (such as boats and cars) versus the intangibles around these items (such as learning or experiences).

All four scenarios in the matrix were focused on how the passions of collectors would evolve over the next decade or so. The clear implication was that if Hagerty did a great job of anticipating and supporting these evolving passions, then the other forces would take care of themselves.

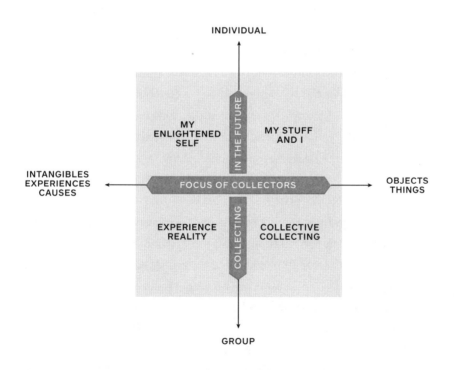

HAGERTY'S SCENARIO MATRIX:
FOUR PATHS FOR THE FUTURE OF COLLECTING

Coming out of the session, Hagerty's leaders agreed on a simple, galvanizing mission and vision summed up in three words: "We fuel collectors." With this renewed clarity of purpose, the firm doubled down on its commitment to the hobby of collecting—through youth programs, web content, new concierge services, public advocacy, and more.

Largely as a result of these investments, Hagerty has enjoyed continued growth ever since—even in the midst of the worst US recession since the Great Depression, and with the financial sector and the Michigan auto industry especially hard hit.

"We made a lot of investments as the economy was heading south because we had our true-north orientation," says Okerstrom. "We kept on investing in what we knew was right at a time when many businesses— especially publicly traded ones—would have quit."

The Hagerty experience shows how good framing can combine with other design choices to enable a strong outcome. By choosing a focal question with a long time horizon and a scenario matrix that emphasized customers' passions, they focused their strategic conversation on the deeper factors driving the success of their business. In this strategic conversation, Hagerty's leaders didn't necessarily learn anything that they didn't already know. Rather, they developed together—through a powerful, shared experience—the confidence to act on their deepest convictions.[7]

FRAMES THAT PROPEL THE CONVERSATION FORWARD

You need to be aware of another frame—and in some ways it's the most critical. After a strategic conversation, the last thing you want is to have the big ahas and all that momentum come to a screeching halt. To stop that from happening, you need an *output frame*. An output frame is the bridge between what happened in the session and what needs to happen next. It creates a through-line from a strategic conversation to the next step in the journey.

Unless you work at a small organization, chances are that only a subset of the people who will be driving your session's results participated in your strategic conversation; many other employees and investors will need to get clued in and on board, too. However, participants often struggle afterward to convey the content and the *feel* of a strategic conversation to those who weren't there, often resorting to slide-show summaries. It's a rare group of people that rallies around a pie chart or gets deeply motivated by a bullet-point battle cry. Good output frames can overcome this challenge by translating the experience and insights of a session through a metaphor, visual, or story that those who weren't there can absorb and use.

If you've just had a strategic conversation for Building Understanding, you may want to come up with something like the Drip and the Avalanche—a "frame of few words" that will enable faster insight that can propel you toward Shaping Choices. If you're designing a strategic conversation for Shaping Choices, then you'll want something like the scenario matrix that the Hagerty leaders created, which provides structure for developing and weighing the main options in a disciplined way.

Creating a "sticky story" can be an especially effective way to ensure the insights of a session live on in an organization. Stories are natural translation tools: they tell what happened in a way that engages our imagination and makes us want to learn more. They're bundles of information put into a logical package, with an emotional wrapping around them. People *get* stories; when you've got a good story, it's much easier for people to follow your logic and share it with others. Stories can go viral in a way that few other forms of communication can.

Stories have another great feature: they're scalable and adaptable to different settings. Think about the leaders of Hagerty. At the end of their strategic conversation, they had a new catchphrase—"We fuel collectors"—that made their future direction and priorities crystal clear. Starting with this kernel of a message, they could then create different stories that would resonate with different audiences.

For employees, they might tell the backstory of the Chicago workshop, to give a sense of how they came to this agreement. For customers, they might connect this catchphrase to their history as a company, tying it back to the founders' initial inspiration to serve the unique needs of collectors.

For shareholders, they might tell a story around the specific investments they plan to make to fuel the passion of collectors, and how these will drive future business success.

As MIT's Michael Schrage, a prominent writer and consultant on strategy and innovation, puts it, "The whole purpose of a strategic conversation is not just to have a good conversation about strategy. It's about getting to a framework for the alignment of behaviors that help you get to the outcomes that you need."[8]

When designing your next strategic conversation, you'll want to spend serious time thinking in advance about both your *input* frames—how you are setting up the problem and content of the session—and the kind of *output* frames you hope to leave with. As your frames get smarter and more evolved, so should the choices and actions your group makes as a result.

SET THE SCENE

Have you ever brought your own plates to a restaurant? How about a bed to a hotel? A seat to an airplane? So why did Darcy Draft and her team at Amway Corporation—a global leader in the direct-selling business, based in Ada, Michigan—haul in furniture to Chicago's Swissôtel, a high-end meeting venue that was already fully appointed?

To shake things up.

"When people walk into a regular meeting, they're expecting a square conference room, maybe some windows, and either a long table or standard round ones," says Draft, a strategic-planning manager at Amway. She wanted to dash those expectations—along with the default "meeting mindset" they tend to trigger. That's because this gathering wasn't just any meeting: it was a strategic conversation on the future of Amway's distributors, a global network of millions of independent business owners.

Draft and her team deliberately chose a funky, triangle-shaped room with obstructing pillars and divided the room into three distinct spaces: a café, a screening room, and a crafts studio. Then they replaced the standard-issue hotel furniture with sofas, easy chairs, and barstools that made the space feel more like a homey den or a neighborhood hangout.

"When people first walked into the room, they said things like 'Oh, this is interesting—what are we doing?'" Draft recalls. "They were immediately taken aback and curious." But she didn't set the scene this way for mere shock value. "If you're going to take somebody out of their current thinking, you need to put them in a different environment and different situations."[1]

While trucking furniture into an odd-shaped hotel space might be an extreme example, it's also a revealing one. Most people, when charged with finding a meeting venue, will ask, Where's a place that has everything we need? Black belt designers of strategic conversations ask instead, Where and how can we create the best environment to support our purpose? Instead of thinking like a project manager or an event planner, they think like a producer and a host.

Black belts fuss over finding the right kind of space—then work hard to make it their own. They bring visual thinking into the program. And like the folks at Amway with their carefully mismatched furniture, they *do* sweat the small stuff—big-time.

KEY PRACTICE 1
MAKE YOUR SPACE

Think for a moment about all the different kinds of restaurants you've been to—just the spaces, without the food or service or patrons. No doubt they're a wide range of environments—from serene to upbeat, cool to warm, traditional to avant garde. Each has a unique mood that in turn affects your own. When you choose a restaurant, it's second nature to consider what kind of setting will fit your purpose. You wouldn't throw a kids' birthday party at a formal French restaurant—or propose marriage at a run-down pizza joint.

So why do so many people choose to hold strategic conversations in spaces that aren't right? In part because finding a workable space is harder than it sounds. Most standard meeting rooms in offices and hotels are either mediocre or terrible. If you want to hear a black belt designer go off on a rant, try asking Corey Ford how he feels about standard meeting spaces.

Ford spends many of his days in strategic conversations around Silicon Valley. He's the managing director for Matter Ventures, a "start-up accelerator" that provides funding and other support to new media entrepreneurs. He's also an Emmy Award–winning producer of documentary films—so he knows what it takes to set a scene.

"The impact of space is huge—but it's probably the most overlooked tool in terms of influencing behavior and impact," says Ford. "I haven't seen many people using space well. They usually fall into whatever the default environment is—typically a formal conference room, with a big-ass table in the middle of it.

"Maybe there's a whiteboard, but usually not. And there are all kinds of physical barriers—screens, furniture, laptops—that cut off people's connection with one another. Plus, there's little or no white space, that makes it hard to generate new ideas. It's a very low-energy environment. Everyone is leaning back."[2]

The scant attention paid to meeting spaces violates not just common sense but reams of research on the ways that space shapes our mood, behavior, and productivity. Access to natural light has been found to boost academic performance, workplace productivity, psychological well-being, and physical health.[3] The color scheme of a room can impact how people approach problems, with blue walls fostering creativity and red ones raising urgency.[4] Cognitive errors increase when the room temperature strays outside optimal range.[5] Moderate levels of ambient noise inspire higher productivity.[6] While it's theoretically *possible* that a breakthrough idea could come out of a windowless conference room with a bland color scheme, bad A/V systems, and bustling traffic outside, we've never heard of it.

GET A "SHELL SPACE" THAT WORKS

A space doesn't have to be loaded with extras to support a strategic conversation—it just has to get the basics right. We think of these basics as making up a *shell space*, which can then be customized for a specific purpose and group.

Building 20 at Massachusetts Institute of Technology (MIT) was a legendary shell space. Designed in one day as a temporary facility for military research during World War II, Building 20 was never given an official name. But it was a campus fixture for fifty-five years, enjoying cult status.

Two words often used to describe Building 20 were *utilitarian* and *spartan*. The three-story, 250,000-square-foot building was sturdy and airy but had little else going for it. The structure was made of wood with a concrete slab for a floor, and cheap, movable walls throughout. It was unburdened by architectural detail or aesthetic flourishes.

The structure was modest, but the insights that sprang from it were anything but. As home to many of the school's experimental and interdisciplinary programs, Building 20 was the site of major breakthroughs in nuclear physics, electromagnetics, linguistics, food technology, and more. Nine Nobel Prize winners toiled under its roof, and numerous tech companies were born there—including Digital Equipment Corporation and Bose Acoustics. Building 20 more than earned its nickname: the Magic Incubator.[7]

What made Building 20 so productive? MIT had scores of better-appointed buildings that weren't nearly as celebrated. By all reports, two main factors were behind the building's success. The first was its flexibility and adaptability. Because the building was "temporary," people felt free to customize their space as needed. They would run wires wherever they wanted, move the walls around, and display artifacts—intellectual and personal—that fueled their creativity. Second, the building featured wide halls and well-placed common areas that encouraged the spontaneous mixing of people and ideas.[8]

When searching for your own shell space, keep the lessons of Building 20 in mind. First and foremost, make sure it gets the basics right, including the flexibility to make it your own.

Many other features are nice to have as well, such as a great view, outdoor spaces for breaks, a setting filled with natural materials such as wood and stone, an energizing color scheme, and nearby restrooms. Our "Room 101" list (see sidebar) provides the basics, and trust us, it can be hard enough to find all of these in one place. Sometimes, to get a good shell space, you've

---

ROOM 101

Here's our checklist of basic room requirements for strategic conversations.

Pick a room that works . . .

▸ *Size:* Doesn't feel cramped or cavernous.

▸ *Shape:* Allows everyone to see and be easily seen.

▸ *Space:* Works well for both plenary and breakout sessions (which may or may not be in separate rooms), with ample open space.

▸ *Windows:* Let the sunshine in!

And can be easily adapted . . .

▸ *Furniture:* Movable, supporting quick set changes as needed.

▸ *Writing surface:* Gives participants space to write, doodle, and work out ideas on paper.

▸ *Clear wall space:* Enough to hang posters, timelines, templates, or other materials that need to be visible at all times.

And is comfortable and free from distractions . . .

▸ *Seating:* Comfy and breathable.

▸ *Room temperature:* Controllable and reasonably set.

▸ *Acoustics:* Everyone can hear everyone else clearly, with no distracting noises in the background.

▸ *Minimal visual distractions:* No visual craziness such as psychedelic carpets, bad art, cluttered storage piles, or busy traffic.

---

got to look beyond the default options found in hotels and office buildings. We've run strategic conversations in all kinds of venues: schools, art galleries, nightclubs, sports stadiums, theaters, and even a convent in Malaysia.

NEXT, MAKE THE SPACE YOUR OWN

Once you have your shell space, you'll want to start shaping it to your purpose. Often, this means adopting a guiding theme or metaphor to help you make choices that hang together.

Remember the folks at Amway? Draft and her team had a rare opportunity to engage a diverse group of leaders on some big issues related to the future needs of their global network of distributors. A couple dozen firm leaders from different parts of the business were flying to Chicago from four continents to participate in that two-day session. In preparation, the team had done research on twenty trend areas—from urbanization to the rise of emerging markets to the changing role of women. With all this content, they knew it would be easy to overwhelm participants with complexity— and doubted that many would have time to wade through a dense pre-reading.

So the team opened the session by immersing participants in a "living pre-read." That's what those three different spaces—café, screening room, and crafts studio—were all about.

Draft's team split participants into three groups of eight and assigned them each to a space. In Café Expertista—the area designed to feel like a local coffeehouse—participants talked informally with three guest experts about socioeconomic change. (The plenary discussions were also held here, to encourage interaction.) In the screening room, participants sat in easy chairs and watched videos of provocative TED talks about emerging business models. Over in the crafts studio, participants hovered over a workbench with scissors and glue sticks, creating thematic collages out of carefully selected articles and images.[9] The Amway team used not one but three organizing metaphors to set their scene. In doing so, they made one of the heaviest parts of most sessions—the content download—more engaging.

You don't always have the luxury of this kind of carte blanche; sometimes you've got to work within tight constraints. That's when it's even more important to get creative.

Gervais Tompkin, a principal at the architecture firm Gensler, once had a client issue an intense mandate: help my group make a month's worth of big design decisions on a new office complex . . . in just four hours.

With little time for discussion and many issues on the docket, the Gensler team cooked up a fun way to signal the importance of making clear choices fast. They branded the session "The Black and White Meeting"—officially banning all shades of gray. Working off an aggressive and rigid agenda, participants were asked to debate each point vigorously, vote, and then move on. To underscore the point, the team made sure that all pre-readings, session materials, and the room itself were cast in black and white. The team's dress code for the day? Black and white only. This two-tone theme set the scene for an efficient decision-making session—with just enough humor to dial back the pressure.[10]

Sometimes, making your space means leaving it behind altogether. Our colleague Eamonn Kelly was once charged with helping the leaders of a sales force find their way through a major shift in circumstances. For years, the company's bestselling product had enjoyed a near-monopoly market position and the high profit margins that came with it. But when the product's patent expired, the sales team was plunged into a world of tough competition.

To help them grasp this new reality, Kelly decided to get the team out of their usual space—literally and figuratively. He took them on a learning journey that included eight sites, each of which had lessons for their situation. Site number four was a casino, where the execs piled out of a bus—and soon found themselves getting schooled in the dark art of draw poker by actress turned celebrity poker player Mimi Rogers.

Rogers gave her students a taste of what sudden, accelerated competition feels like. "She showed them how, when the number of players goes up, the dynamics at the poker table completely change," Kelly says. "When there are more players, the odds of winning each hand change dramatically, so your strategy and bluffing behavior needs to change, too."[11] The lesson was visceral—and the executives quickly absorbed it.

As you make your space for your next strategic conversation, be aware that people are becoming more sophisticated—and demanding—about the environments they inhabit. (Think of how much restaurants, vacation resorts, and shopping malls have changed over the past couple of decades.) This wave of rising expectations about our physical surroundings is washing over our business meetings, too. We've seen increasing pushback from hosts and participants against the sterile, generic venues that still dominate the business-meeting landscape. Sooner or later the time will come when few hosts—or participants—will consider holding an important strategic conversation in such dreary places.

KEY PRACTICE 2
GET VISUAL

People are natural visual thinkers. Field research shows that vision trumps all other senses when it comes to how humans learn and remember—a phenomenon known as *pictorial superiority effect*. "Text and oral presentations are not just less efficient than pictures for retaining certain types of information—they are *way* less efficient," writes cognitive scientist John Medina in his book *Brain Rules*. "If information is presented orally, people remember about 10 percent, tested 72 hours after exposure. That figure goes up to 65 percent if you add a picture." [12]

Black belt designers are always looking for opportunities to engage participants visually. Good visuals can dramatically decrease the time it takes people to reach insights and come to agreement. Too often, though, visuals are underleveraged, poorly used, or both. Tapping into the full power of visuals takes a bit more thought and effort than sprinkling a presentation with clip art.

For a strategic conversation, you have at least six kinds of visuals to think about, listed in the following sidebar. Almost every effective strategic conversation we're aware of featured some combination of these elements. The key is to be thoughtful about which ones to use—where, when, why, and how.

THE POWER OF SEEING THE SAME THING AT THE SAME TIME

Visuals are not just memorable. They help people collaborate better by making ideas concrete. Because strategic conversations involve adaptive challenges that are open-ended and intertwined, it's usually hard to know where and how to begin. Smart use of visuals is often the best way to help a group cut into the issues and start making progress.

VISUAL ELEMENTS TO A STRATEGIC CONVERSATION

The most common visual elements that black belts employ in their strategic conversations, roughly ordered from fixed (created in advance) to more emergent (created live), are:[13]

▸ *Prepared materials:* All premade materials that put a visual stamp on a session, such as slides, posters, handouts, or timelines.

▸ *Process templates:* Worksheets or templates designed to help guide participants through a series of steps.

▸ *Frameworks:* Visual models that help structure conversation and connect individual issues to a larger challenge; these can be as simple as a timeline or as complex as a systems diagram.

▸ *Prototypes:* Drawings or other renderings of working-draft ideas and solutions; these can be low resolution or highly polished, created in advance or live.

▸ *Live capture:* Flip charts, graphic recordings, photographs, and digital interfaces (such as a wiki) that capture and curate content in real time.

▸ *Emergent sketches:* Any visual interface used for real-time exploration and idea building, such as mind mapping, doodling, or a graffiti wall.

As we discussed in the last chapter, the modern history of strategic thinking can be traced largely through a succession of "sticky" visual frameworks. The BCG Growth-Share Matrix, Porter's Five Forces, and McKinsey's three horizons of growth are all ideas that can quickly be sketched out, applied to a current situation, and shared with others.

In the story about Toyota Financial Services, we shared the more recent visual framework of the Business Model Generation Canvas and its nine key elements to designing a business model. This "canvas" actually looks more like a jigsaw puzzle showing how the elements fit together as a system of interdependent parts. It's a canvas in the sense that you use it to create your own pictures of what your new business model could look like.

It can be hard for a group to get its collective head around something as complex as a business model, which includes such diverse elements as cost structure, customer segments, distribution channels, and revenue streams.[14] The power of the canvas is that it forces people to explain their ideas clearly and to connect them to one another. Without a visual map of some sort, most groups will wander aimlessly around a long list of issues, without closing on any of them.

"My biggest learning over the last three years is that these visuals are not just a nice-to-have," says Alexander Osterwalder, coauthor of *Business Model Generation.* "They are core to why these tools actually work in strategic conversations—in understanding how a business model works and in explaining it to somebody else. In workshops, I can always see the difference between when people are just talking and when they are using the visual tool of the canvas." [15]

Another common tool for getting visual in strategic conversations is graphic recording—drawing key points as they're spoken for everyone to see. Done well, this kind of visual capture delivers far more benefits than just note-taking in the background. Participants get direct and immediate feedback that they're being heard, which can lower their stress and make them more receptive to others' ideas. Key points and insights are made visible and available—making it more likely that they'll get picked up again later. The hand-drawn style of most graphic recorders also adds a warm, human touch that makes the session feel more informal and conversational. And the visual record of the session can often live on and spark further conversations afterward in ways that executive summaries and other reports rarely do.[16]

"The work is eye-catching—it draws you in," says Gretchen Gscheidle, director of insight and exploration at Herman Miller, the workplace design company, which often uses graphic recording at its strategic conversations. "I've used it to brief people who were not at a workshop and, in particular, people visiting from our international divisions," says Gscheidle. "The visuals help them feel closer to the work of that day rather than just listening to me talk about it." [17]

Dan Roam—bestselling author of *The Back of the Napkin* and *Blah, Blah,*

Blah—spends much of his time helping organizations draw their way out of tough challenges, using a process he calls *napkining*. "The notion is that thinking becomes different when it's not locked in my mind anymore," Roam says. "It becomes this thing in between us. By putting it in a picture, it becomes real in a way that forces us to think more clearly about the problem." [18]

His approach—like many visual methods—draws on the concept of distributed cognition, which argues that groups have thought processes that are distinct from those of the individuals within them. [19] When you get ideas out of people's heads and onto the page, strategic conversations can become much more real—and more productive.

VISUALIZING A NEW GLOBAL WORKPLACE—IN FIVE DAYS

The topic of workplace design may not make your pulse race, but it's an important one for most organizations. Real estate and related costs are a major line item in most operating budgets. The way that an office is laid out can dramatically affect employee productivity and profitability. The look and feel of a workplace can do a lot to define—or undermine—a firm's image with customers, partners, and employees. Choices about where people sit and what amenities they have access to can throw off a surprising amount of heat. After all, many people spend about half their waking hours at the office.

The architecture firm Gensler helps organizations of all kinds wrestle with these challenges. A few years back, a global manufacturing company gave Gensler the following *Mission: Impossible* assignment: define global workplace design guidelines that could work for tens of thousands of employees across a wide range of markets and cultures—and get most of the job done in one five-day session. Participants included key regional leaders plus experts on such topics as technology, HR, and branding.

Much of Gensler's work focuses on the connection between space and productivity, and their office offered a perfect shell space for the occasion: an open, airy room with natural brick, lots of sunlight, and plenty of usable wall space. What really made the difference at this session, though, was how they brought visual thinking into the program.

The project was led by Gervais Tompkin, of "The Black and White Meeting" fame. Tompkin and the team decided the only way they could make the needed progress in five days was through rapid-fire prototyping. The organizing metaphor they chose for the session was a *charrette*—a term that dates to the École des Beaux-Arts in nineteenth-century Paris. The word means "cart" and refers to the method of creating art by rapid iteration under extreme deadline pressure. (When the cart arrived at a student's station, time was up.) This *charrette* process was used to develop two outputs simultaneously: a set of written policy guidelines and accompanying illustrations. Says Tompkin, "We were constantly going back and forth between words, images, and diagrams to express and share ideas" throughout the program.

As in any long session, energy levels rose and fell. The first couple days were spent establishing core principles and other baseline understanding. On Wednesday, with many issues outstanding and the Friday deadline looming, some participants were growing skeptical about getting to decisions—and worried about what they would report when they went back home.

At this point Tompkin's drawing board went from a nice-to-have to a necessity. When the group became frustrated by lack of clarity or consensus on an issue, Tompkin would bring it back to ground-level reality with a series of day-in-the-life sketches. If a participant had a hard time seeing how a given design choice would play out in practice, Tompkin would listen to the concerns—then whip out his pens, interpreting the proposed guidelines for offices in places as different as Germany and Japan, Brazil and India.

"I was just cranking out these drawings and testing them with the group, asking, 'Is *this* what you're talking about?' until they had images that fit with their perspectives," Tompkin recalls. Given how fast he was working, the sketches were low resolution—and good enough. In this way, participants worked through most of their outstanding issues and reached consensus around a set of policies that struck a good balance between global consistency and regional flexibility.[20]

The group left the session with lots of forward momentum that wouldn't have been achieved without a visually rich, in-person strategic conversation. It's inconceivable they would have gotten anywhere near the same level of agreement by e-mail and conference calls alone—especially in five days. If they'd met for a week without the visual support, they would likely have left with a "high-level agreement" that would have evaporated as their planes headed home. The visual prototypes enabled participants to truly see their ideas come together, in a way that accelerated action afterward.

KEY PRACTICE 3
DO SWEAT THE SMALL STUFF

If you ever have the misfortune of spending time in prison but get the chance to make your case for parole, try to get a hearing first thing in the morning—or right after lunch. Your freedom may depend on it. That's what a team of researchers from Columbia University and Ben-Gurion University of the Negev discovered.

The team put 1,112 parole hearings conducted in Israel in 2009 under a statistical microscope and found a stunning result. On average, the odds of a favorable outcome for the parolee started at 65 percent with the first case in the day and fell steadily to near zero odds just before lunch. After lunch, the odds were reset at 65 percent and again fell back to nothing over the afternoon (with another upward spike after a short afternoon break). If your parole hearing appeared on the docket at 9:00 a.m. or 1:00 p.m., your odds of walking away free were about two to one. But if your number came up at 11:45 a.m. or 4:45 p.m., it was basically hopeless.

With this large sample size, the researchers tested their result for every imaginable explanation—discrimination, difficulty of cases, and so on. They were left with just one plausible answer: after enough time without a break or food, judges get tired and cranky, which affects their judgment.

There's no reason to think this result is limited to Israeli judges. As the authors point out, the study measures a fundamental biological and psychological effect (known as "mental depletion") that may hold true for any group of people making decisions over a long period of time.[21]

While the media jumped on these findings, they shouldn't surprise anyone who's run a few strategic conversations. We've all seen how the small stuff—such as how recently participants last ate or had a break—can alter mood and behavior and change the outcome of a session. The Israeli judges study proves just how big a deal the small stuff can be.

A HEALTHY CASE OF OCD

Obsessive attention to detail is a hallmark of all great design—whether it's the way the parts of a BMW come together, the seamless experiences of a great Broadway production, or the intricate details of Notre Dame Cathedral in Paris. Steve Jobs of Apple was renowned for his insistence that all parts of the Apple system—devices, software interfaces, and retail experiences—be elegant, integrated, and consistent. Designers of strategic conversation are no different. They know that little details matter. So they fret over them, always scanning for opportunities to shrink risk factors and improve participants' experiences.

One major risk in any session is distraction. While strategic conversations bear little resemblance to parole hearings, they're similar in one important respect: most people find them physically and mentally exhausting. Strategic conversations require extended periods of focused concentration—a rarity in our age of hyperactive multitasking. People will often jump at any excuse to shift their attention elsewhere.

Here's a scenario you're trying to avoid. A key participant doesn't have a pen so she steps outside the room to look for one. Once out of the room, she peeks at her smartphone and discovers that someone wants to talk with her. She decides to make a "quick" call, after which she realizes she needs to go to the bathroom, and . . . before you know it, you've lost a half hour of attention from a key participant, who now can't follow the conversation. All for not having a simple pen handy.

One of the most common distractions we see is the lunch delivery that arrives at 11:30 a.m. in advance of a noon break. This may sound like an innocuous misstep, but it can become a minor disaster. If that food is put down somewhere visible—especially if it's warm and smells good—it's almost guaranteed that half your group will mentally drift away, their minds and stomachs now set on lunch. By not taking the small stuff seriously, you've lost a half hour of productivity.

Black belt designers are tenacious about hunting down and banishing all sources of distraction. This means getting to the venue ahead of time and developing a sudden case of obsessive-compulsive disorder over things you normally think of as trivial. It means making sure that all equipment and supplies are in place; the room temperature is moderate; the furniture is comfortable; nearby noise levels are low; and food will be delivered at a reasonable time and place.

But sweating the small stuff isn't just about managing risk. As we've discussed, strategic conversations tend to make people uncomfortable. The issues are complex and sometimes even threatening. Participants are on the spot to perform, often in a politically charged environment. So, to get the best results out of a session, you want to take steps to reduce these sources of discomfort.

To help your guests feel comfortable, choose a cozy venue with a nice view or an appropriate gift of some sort. But by far the biggest tool in your box is food. Participants tend to get ravenously hungry at strategic conversations—because the work is so mental that it's physical, and because people get antsy from being cooped up for long periods. As a result, many people eat more than usual at these sessions, which makes food choices all the more important.

We could devote a whole chapter to food, but will restrain ourselves to one piece of advice: find ways to comfort people with food without resorting to "comfort foods" loaded with simple carbohydrates, such as pasta or sweets. Simple carbohydrates are the mortal enemy of strategic conversations because they lead to sugar crashes that sap people's energy. When choosing your group's menu, find ways to pamper them with food that boosts their energy instead of depleting it.

THE DELIGHT IS IN THE DETAILS

Since it's not possible to dwell on every tiny detail, you'll want to think carefully about which ones matter most to setting your scene. At the Gensler session, the team created an enormous, poster-size copy of the five-day agenda so that the group always knew where they were in the process. The team made life-size cardboard cutouts of imaginary characters to keep front of mind key constituents who couldn't be in the room. They also compiled a music sound track—a mix of up-tempo electronica and bossa nova tunes—to create a sense of forward movement and to serve as an "aural curtain" to signal intermissions in the program.

The Amway team chose different details to focus on (in addition to the furniture). They brought in a chalkboard for illustrating ideas in Café Expertista—similar to the kind where you'd find a menu of espresso drinks. They created a signature image (futureINsight) for all session materials, to create a sense of continuity across the varied experiences. They gave participants branded coffee tumblers to use at the session and take home as a daily reminder of the experience.

In sweating the small stuff, work to make sure all elements of the environment are congruent with your purpose and overall design. When you get the small stuff right, people notice it—often subconsciously—in a way that increases their engagement and confidence. When you mess it up, people *really* notice it—in a way that can undermine their trust in you and in the process.

NO EXCUSES: TAKING PERSONAL RESPONSIBILITY FOR YOUR GROUP'S EXPERIENCE

We realize some of the stories in this chapter may feel a bit "out there." Not everyone has access to a dedicated special-events team to attend to every detail (like Amway), serious visual-design talent (like Gensler), or the budget to bring in a celebrity poker instructor.

No matter. You can do lots of small things to set the scene—in any space and with any budget. It doesn't cost much to show a few provocative videos that stoke creativity, inject some customer perspective through video or audio commentary, or take the group on a walking break in a nearby park. When you think like a producer and a host, you'll find plenty of "cheap and cheerful" options like these.

Sometimes, you just have to work with a venue that's far from ideal. When this happens, find a way to embrace the constraints.

Bernie Jaworski—a faculty member (and Peter Drucker chair) at Claremont Graduate School—once walked into the venue for a strategic conversation he was running only to find a windowless "bowling alley." The room was so long and narrow that, in any standard arrangement, people sitting at the round tables at one end wouldn't be able to see or hear people at the other.

After a few hushed curses, Jaworski got down to work. He shoved the tables aside and moved the seats into a theater-in-the-round arrangement with a space in the middle where the presenters and facilitators would take turns "onstage." In a few minutes—and without spending a dime—he transformed a room that was built for distraction into a space for dialogue. By simply rearranging the furniture, Jaworski embodied the spirit of host and producer by taking personal responsibility for his group's experience.[22]

Setting the scene well can take a lot of work. Is it worth all the effort? Darcy Draft of Amway is sure of it. "At the end of the day," she says, "I'd much rather have people talking about Amway and our strategy than that the service was crappy, I had a bad seat, and we had no windows."[23]

Looking back eighteen months later, Draft says, people at Amway are still talking about their session in Chicago. "We got together to talk about the future of business ownership and think about a ten-year plan for our global sales group," she says. "But after it was over, we realized we had unlocked key questions about our entire business, which are now helping to shape our long-term strategic direction."

MAKE IT AN EXPERIENCE

No offense, but your memory stinks. That's okay—so does ours. Human memory is notoriously buggy. On rigorous testing, eyewitness accounts—even ones we are dead sure of—often prove hopelessly unreliable. In his book *The Seven Sins of Memory*, Harvard psychologist Daniel Schacter shows how several key aspects of memory are both positive features and "bugs" (flaws) at the same time. High on this list of features/bugs is the brain's ability to go into autopilot mode when doing rote tasks that require minimal attention, such as driving a car or washing the dishes.[1]

Autopilot is awesome. Because of it, we can multitask and get a lot of routine things done at the same time. It also helps us prioritize stimuli—if we didn't have autopilot, we'd have to pay total attention to everything around us. But autopilot mode also has a downside: we can easily miss important things while our brain is on cruise control.

Imagine you're wandering around your house doing chores and suddenly can't find your glasses. You put them down and then forgot where. Actually, because you were on autopilot when you put your glasses down, you never knew where you put them. In technical terms, as you put your glasses down, you didn't *encode* this information in your brain. You can't forget something that you never knew in the first place.[2]

Why is this relevant to strategic conversations? Because we spend a lot of time on autopilot every day—and standard meetings practically beg people to go there. A familiar meeting room full of the usual coworkers armed with giant slide decks might as well be an engraved invitation for our brains to tune out. Our bodies may be in the room together, but at any point at your average meeting, it's guaranteed that several—if not most—people's minds are drifting far away.

Think fast: What did you have for lunch six weeks ago today? We'd be astonished if you can recall. Think fast again: What were three key points from the last standard meeting you attended? Depending on how recent that was, you might do better on this question than the last one. We've heard quite a few people struggle to describe the contents of major meetings—even ones that happened just a few days earlier.

If a strategy meeting takes place but nobody remembers its main points just weeks later, did it really happen? Call us dreamers, but we think that strategic conversations about the future of your organization should be a lot more memorable than your average lunch. Probably the most common complaint that we hear about strategy meetings is lack of follow-up. But how are people supposed to act on something they can barely remember?

AN AGENDA IS NOT AN EXPERIENCE

As we've discussed, most people approach a strategic conversation as if it's an important meeting, rather than a distinct genre. They tend to think about the session's agenda in two ways.

The first is as a *systematic march through the relevant content.* From this perspective, crafting the agenda is a matter of identifying and prioritizing all the topics that need to be addressed. However, when faced with an adaptive challenge—such as the puzzling decline of a business model—this approach makes a dangerous assumption. It assumes that if you just work through the topics in a logical sequence—using the best data and tools at your disposal—you'll find your answers. It assumes that you can analyze your way stepwise through adaptive challenges. But such challenges don't lend themselves to technical solutions. They're more like wicked riddles than complex math problems.

The second is as a *balancing act of internal interests.* Strategic conversations involve a good deal of posturing and jockeying for position among participants, even if it's good-natured. When preparing for an important session, meeting organizers will spend a fair amount of time navigating these dynamics in advance, so as to manage them effectively in the room. The agenda will inevitably reflect some compromise between various interests—a half hour for Bob's pet topic, an hour for Janet's, and so on.

Both of these approaches are important. Every strategic conversation needs a firm grounding in relevant content—but focusing too much on data and slides will limit your ability to connect with your group. You also need to immerse yourself in personal and group dynamics—but focusing on personalities too much can lead to a compromise that keeps the peace but doesn't generate breakthroughs.

When planning a strategic conversation's agenda, your primary goal should be to *create a powerful, shared experience.* This way you can strike the right balance between your content and your people.

This focus on experience may sound counterintuitive. Many people think of "experience" as a nice-to-have additional layer—such as kicking off a session with a pleasant dinner, finding a great off-site venue, or making sure the meeting materials look pretty. But the experience of a strategic conversation means much more than this. It means looking at the session as a psychological and emotional journey as much as an intellectual one.

In the first chapter, we shared the moment when Pierre Wack realized that he needed to get inside the heads of Shell's managers if he wanted his strategic conversations to have impact. In this chapter, we extend Wack's insight: you must get inside their hearts and guts as well. The best way to do this is by creating an experience.

Below, we briefly introduce two strategic conversations where a powerful participant experience led to a moment of impact. Imagine that you're the one responsible for designing a two-day Building Understanding session in both cases.

▸ Situation 1: Embracing the mobile future at a major software company. *Intuit is a leading provider of accounting software for small businesses, with about $4 billion in revenue in 2012. In 2010, company leaders realized they were not yet providing enough software applications for mobile platforms such as smartphones and tablets, which were taking off in popularity. While the need for a shift was clear, mobile platforms did not have a natural home in any of the existing product divisions—indeed, they could be seen as competing for investment resources. Founder Scott Cook and CEO Brad Smith decided to organize a strategic conversation for the firm's top eighteen executives to discuss the need for a stronger mobile presence—and to start working toward a solution.*

▸ Situation 2: Dealing with declining numbers at a major Catholic order. *The De La Salle Christian Brothers are the second-largest teaching order in the Catholic Church (after the Jesuits), with about six thousand vowed Brothers working in hundreds of schools, colleges, and universities in more than eighty countries. As with many other orders, the Brothers are declining in number every year as new recruits fail to replace those retiring or passing away. In 2002, leaders of the order from across Australia, New Zealand, and Papua New Guinea came together to discuss how to adapt to this reality. At stake was the future of a few dozen schools—many of them dedicated to providing opportunities for less fortunate kids. In two days, their goal was to gain clarity and commitment on safeguarding these important works despite the Brothers' declining numbers.*

How would you approach these sessions? What kinds of experiences might help these organizations move forward? We'll come back to these examples in a bit.

KEY PRACTICE 1
DISCOVER, DON'T TELL

One of the biggest complaints we hear about meetings is how much time is spent sitting and listening to speakers march through their slide decks. Serious research shows that people have a remarkable cognitive immunity against learning from presentations—even when they want to. So why do we spend so much time on them?

Part of the reason is habit and tradition. By the time you enter professional life, you've spent thousands of hours in school listening to lectures, from grade school through graduate school. It's still the dominant model for teaching today: sit people down, ask them to open their eyes and ears, and pour in information and knowledge.

This traditional approach is under heavy fire from some leading educators. Prominent among them is Carl Wieman, a Nobel Prize–winning physicist who teaches at the University of British Columbia. For years, Wieman's been waging a campaign to persuade his colleagues to apply the scientific method of inquiry to the teaching of science. He's appalled that, despite dramatic gains in both technology and our knowledge about how people learn, the dominant mode of teaching remains one-way lectures delivered by a "sage on the stage."

Wieman and his colleagues have conducted rigorous research on students' ability to retain information from lectures, and their results are consistently discouraging. Even right after a lecture is over, studies show that students remember almost nothing of what was said. It's as if they came out of a screening of *Eternal Sunshine of the Spotless Mind*, still rubbing their eyes. Lectures are so bad at communicating information that at the end of a semester, many undergraduates understand *less* about basic concepts in physics than they did going in. And these are good students at top schools.[3]

Lectures don't work for two reasons: (1) they overload listeners with more information than their brains can handle at one time; and (2) the listeners are passive. Wieman compares their continued use today to the practice of bloodletting in medieval medicine. By contrast, what does work, in study after study, is *experiential learning*—enabling people to discover key insights and concepts for themselves, with a bit of guidance.

Joe Redish, a physics professor at the University of Maryland, helps students learn Newton's second law of motion by dropping two balls of different weights simultaneously from a second-story window. Intuition tells us that the heavier ball should land first, but Newton's law says that's wrong. When the two balls hit the ground at the same time, Newton's law becomes hard to forget, long after the formula has faded from memory. Lessons learned from vivid experiences such as this are fiendishly hard to unlearn.[4]

Presentations don't work; experiential learning does. Yet current "best" practice for sharing information in most high-stakes strategy discussions is the same as the university lecture: a slide presentation delivered to a passive audience. What were the three main points of the last presentation you sat through? What was the *topic*, even?

EMBRACING THE MOBILE FUTURE AT INTUIT

Let's pick up the story of Intuit and its conundrum. The year is 2010 and the world is moving fast toward mobile platforms—a bit faster than Intuit is. While the shift is opening many opportunities for the firm, there are potential threats, too. If Intuit waits too long to embrace the shift, it could lose market share to well-funded, fast-moving start-ups. But these platforms haven't proved profitable in the marketplace yet, making the move appear expensive and risky—at least in the short term.

The stakes are high, the participants have mixed motives, and just lecturing them about the most recent data on key trends probably won't spur them to agreement and action. Imagine that you've got two days of precious time with the firm's top eighteen executives. What would you do?

If you're Kaaren Hanson, vice president for the Design Innovation Group at Intuit, you start thinking about how to create a powerful learning experience. An experience that will make the issue real for executives who have heard a lot about the mobile lifestyle but aren't yet living it every day.

Hanson and her team designed a two-day total-immersion program that included a number of familiar elements. The session opened with firm leaders setting the strategic context, followed by presentations on mobile trends and visits from a few executives from other companies that had already made the move to mobile platforms. A few live "mobile first" customers—entrepreneurs who had switched to using mobile phones as their main business platform—also dropped by to interact with the execs in small groups.

But the real moment of impact at the session—and what made it unforgettable—took place far outside the meeting room.

According to Joseph O'Sullivan—a design director at Intuit who organized much of the effort—the team knew its program had to include a visceral experience of the emerging mobile future—not just a "demo" of new mobile functions. "We wanted to put them into a mildly stressful situation where they had to utilize all aspects of a mobile phone to get something done," O'Sullivan says.

After considering several options, the team decided to design a scavenger hunt, using the main street of Half Moon Bay—a seaside town south of San Francisco, where the session was held—as their game board. Participants were divided into five groups and given customized iPhones and Android phones to use in tracking down hidden clues, with each group following a similar but differently sequenced itinerary. Then they were sent out of the hotel to find their way through the hunt.

For ninety minutes the groups raced about town chasing down their clues. To locate a geocache hidden in a bunch of bushes, they used a military-grade GPS application. They used the Word Lens app to translate a clue that was given in Spanish. At a bakery, they used the Foodspotting app to upload pictures of different dishes—and to find their next clue hidden in one of the reviews posted there. At a wine bar, they scanned labels using the RedLaser app to read reviews and add to them. Along the way, they "checked in" with Foursquare to trade comments with the other groups.

"Our goal was to break the frame and make clear that the phone is so much more than a phone," O'Sullivan says. In rapid-fire succession, participants used their phones as a GPS device, a camera, a credit card, a bar-code scanner, a recording device, and a language translator—all relatively new functions at the time. What's more, the hunt showed that familiar activities—such as enjoying a glass of wine—could be enriched by mobile access to an outside world of information and social engagement.

A bit of friendly competition helped bring the scavenger hunt alive as the teams raced to complete the course first—even though they were instructed to take their time. "People got unbelievably competitive," Hanson recalls. But they were also enlightened. "When they arrived at the debrief, they were all excited, saying things like 'Wow, I had no idea my phone could do all this!'"

O'Sullivan recalls, "Getting them out of the hotel and into the town and using the phone in a real-world context was the catalyzing moment. You can intellectualize a presentation. But using the apps this way was key to understanding that the future is here—now. Even the most jaded person who thought they understood mobile felt like they learned something new."

Not many companies would launch their top executives on a scavenger hunt as a way to wrestle with a big strategic issue. What if the head of marketing had found the exercise trivial? What if the CFO returned from it more annoyed than energized?

That's where preparation comes in. "We test the hell out of these experiences until we know that they are going to deliver the ahas reliably," says Hanson, adding that the team worked through about ten iterations of the scavenger hunt before nailing it. On game day, it took a serious logistics crew to make sure everything went as planned. "For the participants, it's magic. For us, it's just hard work."

That hard work paid off. After the session, firm leaders got behind mobile technology in a big way, launching a full suite of products that enabled small-business owners to operate on the go—from mobile payment solutions to payroll management to tax filing. In the two years that followed, revenue from mobile products rose from negligible to about $70 million a year, with CEO Brad Smith declaring the category a critical source of future growth.[5]

While many factors contributed to this outcome, the executive scavenger hunt was among the most memorable. It was so effective and popular that the company decided to repeat the program for the top eighty executives, to deepen the commitment to mobile technology across the organization.

From all our research and experience, sessions that are designed as shared learning experiences can lead to huge impacts—much more than standard meetings. So why don't more people approach their mission-critical strategic conversations this way?

"I think that people just aren't used to it," says Hanson. "It feels very risky—what if it doesn't work? But once you've done it, you cannot go back.

"Inertia is the most powerful force in the universe. If you're sitting in a room with a bunch of slide decks, there's very little that can go wrong. There's just very little that can go right, too."[6]

KEY PRACTICE 2
ENGAGE THE WHOLE PERSON

When faced with a crucial decision, is it better to rigorously examine the data or rely on your intuition?

On the side of data-based decision-making stand countless MBA programs and a consulting industry primed to crank out recommendations based on rigorous analytics. On the side of gut decision-making stand a legion of heroic CEOs—from Steve Jobs to Jack Welch—and bestselling author Malcolm Gladwell, whose book *Blink: The Power of Thinking Without Thinking* promotes the benefits of winging it.[7]

But it's a false choice. Making decisions by data alone—even if it were possible—runs the risk of either "paralysis by analysis" or of making decisions that are logical on the surface but don't work in reality. At the same time, the thought of leaders simply following their guts without a strong reality check is equally terrifying. The last thing that leaders need in navigating VUCA World is an excuse to not think too hard.

It's a dilemma that goes back to the ancient Greeks. For a long time, many scholars saw reason and emotion as separate, often warring, systems. But the scientific study of human emotion—a shockingly young field—has made remarkable gains over the past couple of decades.[8] While there's much we still don't understand, researchers have made important discoveries in recent years that have implications for strategic conversations.

THE IRRATIONALITY OF PURE REASON

In his book *Descartes' Error: Emotion, Reason, and the Human Brain,* neuroscientist Antonio Damasio tells the story of a remarkable patient he calls Elliot, whose life had been saved by surgery that removed an orange-size tumor from his brain. By all outward appearances, Elliot walked away from the experience a lucky man. Despite some damage to his frontal lobe, he suffered no obvious losses in mental or physical capacity. After his recovery, Elliot's mobility, memory, language skills, and reasoning ability were all intact. To a trained medical professional, there was nothing wrong with him.

Yet by the time Damasio met him—in his thirties, a few years after the surgery—Elliot's career was in tatters and his marriage had collapsed. Attempts at new jobs and relationships were equally disastrous. This highly educated and once successful man was now indigent and rudderless.

Damasio's job was to figure out why Elliot's life had collapsed so thoroughly without any visible cause. As any good scientist would, he ran Elliot through a gauntlet of tests. Tests for IQ, language ability, memory, personality disorders, spatial orientation, formal reasoning, and moral judgment. Elliot scored average or better on all of them. Damasio was baffled: he couldn't find a cognitive or psychological test to stump this guy.

In the end, Damasio was left with two firm observations. First, by all reports—including Elliot's—his life had fallen apart because of a string of terrible decisions. He had failed to honor commitments to his family and colleagues, trusted people he shouldn't have, and made choices that appeared random. Second, while his personality was otherwise unchanged postsurgery, there was one notable difference: his emotions were significantly flattened. Even when telling his tragic life story, Elliot's delivery was so lifeless that it was as if he were speaking of another person. While he understood what had happened, the full extent of his own tragedy just didn't register emotionally.

After an exhaustive search for the cause of his patient's woes, Damasio's conclusion was that *Elliot's loss of the ability to feel emotions had so impaired his judgment that he could no longer make sound decisions.* Though his intellect and reason remained perfectly intact—indeed, well above average—he could no longer make even the simplest choices successfully.

Although unable to help Elliot return his life to normal, Damasio has spent the past few decades trying to understand how and why emotions and reason support (or fail to support) each other. Other cases similar to Elliot's have since surfaced—people with brain injuries that impaired only their emotions and their ability to make decisions. For many, the effect was so severe that they were totally paralyzed by minor choices such as what shirt to wear or what to eat for lunch.

Scientists are still working to understand the exact mechanisms by which emotion shapes decision-making. But clearly, reason and emotion are deeply intertwined. Even if we were able to separate the two, the results would be dreadful.[9]

THE EMOTIONAL DESIGN OF STRATEGIC CONVERSATIONS

Designers have long understood that reason and emotion are interconnected. In his classic book *The Design of Everyday Things*, cognitive psychologist and design theorist Don Norman shows in detail how great designs—of products, buildings, or services—engage and delight their users as whole people.[10]

Think about one of your favorite possessions. It could be your car, a tool, a piece of technology, an item of clothing—or even your house. Why do you like it? Your reasons are probably a mixture of head and heart factors. Maybe it's your outdoor barbecue grill. You like its sleek lines, the way it consistently delivers an even heat, and the memories it carries of countless family feasts. While you could sort these factors into separate buckets, your fondness for the grill comes from the total experience of it.

The best strategic conversations are like this, too. They engage your head and your gut equally, and you're not asked to make choices between the two. A common assumption is that we should keep our passions out of important meetings, as unchecked emotions can bring out our worst instincts and subject us to all kinds of biases. But a roomful of hyperrational Mr. Spocks can't solve an adaptive challenge.

When designing a strategic conversation, ask, How can we best engage participants as whole people? How can we tap into their logical *and* emotional selves in a way that leads to smarter choices and action?

CONFRONTING DECLINING NUMBERS AT A CATHOLIC TEACHING ORDER

The De La Salle Christian Brothers are one of the largest teaching orders in the Catholic Church. They operate hundreds of schools, universities, and educational works serving more than 900,000 students in more than a thousand schools and other institutions across more than eighty countries, with a strong preference for serving the poor. Around the world—and for almost three centuries—the Brothers have provided countless people with a quality education grounded in a strong moral and spiritual foundation.[11]

But their numbers are declining every year, due to the aging of the order and a long, steady decrease in new vocations, or recruits. As compelling as their history and mission are, the traditional vows of poverty, chastity, and obedience just aren't the talent magnet they used to be.

In 2002, leaders of the Christian Brothers' regional operations across Australia, New Zealand, and Papua New Guinea (referred to as the District) needed to come up with a plan for ensuring the continued vitality of their work. At the time, seventy-nine active Brothers were working in eighteen schools across the three-country District—many of them focused on helping poor or troubled kids.

A Catholic order is not your average business organization, to put it mildly. Imagine working at a place where you and your peers are committed to the organization for life. An organization where you all came up through the same formative training as young adults. An organization where, after the workday is done, you go home to find your coworkers there, too. In short, an organization where work, family, community, and social life are all blended together into a lifelong commitment and identity.

The elected head of the District at the time (who holds the title *visitor*) was Brother David Hawke, a New Zealander with a warm, pastoral style. The auxiliary visitor, or next-in-line leader, was Ambrose Payne, a pragmatic idealist with keen operational skills who was also principal at a high school in a suburb of Sydney with a large immigrant population.

Brothers David and Ambrose knew that to create meaningful strategies for the future of the District, all Brothers would need to take their declining numbers more seriously. They also knew this would be a challenge, given the Brothers' natural tendency to avoid problems or leave them for leadership to solve.

Working closely with Brothers David and Ambrose, the project team designed a three-day strategic conversation for two dozen leaders across the District, including three lay partners (i.e., non-Brother colleagues). "Please understand that this event is not just another planning session," wrote Brother David in his invitation note to participants. "No less is at stake here than the future health and vitality of the Lasallian mission in the District." The session, held in March 2002 in Narooma, Australia—a quiet beach town a couple hundred miles south of Sydney—included a number of familiar strategy and planning activities, and two key experiential elements.

Much of the first day consisted of level-setting activities, such as reviewing current trends data and prioritizing key issues. The first "experience" came after dinner, when the group watched the award-winning documentary *Breaking the Silence: The Story of the Sisters at DeSales Heights*. The film tells the story of the dismantling of a 150-year-old monastery in West Virginia. It follows twelve elderly nuns as they prepare to leave the only life they have known as adults and enter an uncertain future outside. The film shows the pain of a group of devoted women realizing that the role they've played their entire lives is no longer valued.

While the Brothers sat stoically through the screening of this brutally sad film, the few lay partners present seemed very affected; some were in tears. After it ended, the group went to bed without conversation. This was intense input that they needed to sleep on.

The next day, after a debrief discussion of the film, came the main event: a simulation game called Demography in Action. The objective of the game was to adapt, in real time, to the expected retirements of twenty-four Brothers—about one-third of the active Brothers working in the District's eighteen schools—scheduled in quick succession over the next eight years.

Participants were divided into three teams of eight players each. Each team assumed the role of the District Council (leadership team), with one member playing the role of visitor with final decision rights. Each team played out the events of the coming eight years on a large, colorful, hand-drawn game board showing a map of every location across the District where the Brothers worked. The "pieces" to this game board were the seventy-nine active Brothers, each represented by a cheerful (and nameless) cartoonlike character, with an estimated retirement date shown at his feet.

The teams were given a few minutes to review the expected retirements and form a draft plan. Then a bell rang, announcing that a year had passed—forcing each team to remove from the board all Brothers with a 2003 retirement date. The teams were given a short time to respond to the retirements—either by closing or merging institutions, moving Brothers around, promoting lay partners to leadership roles, or keeping things as they were. This activity was repeated eight times—once for each year from 2003 to 2010—but with decreasing amounts of response time, to turn up the intensity and create the sense of time slipping away.

To the project team's surprise, the energy in the room was extremely high. The groups were actually having fun working through the implications of their own decline.

"The game shocked everybody," Brother Ambrose recalls. "It captured everyone's imagination and freed up the situation. Once you get into the domain of play, there's an opportunity to break through how people normally think about their challenges." By taking a shapeless, depressing fact and converting it into a game where the group could take action, the experience made a challenge that they'd been avoiding much more approachable.

During a debrief discussion afterward, participants made the very observations that the game was designed to evoke. All three teams reported variations on three core insights. The first was "We need to prioritize our energy better and stop spreading ourselves too thin." The second: "If we act sooner, we'll be in better shape and have more choices later." The third: "If you don't have a good game plan going in, you keep getting hit with surprises."

Though the teams had made quite different choices during the game, they didn't bother debating which of their quickly drawn plans was "better." They understood that—at this point in their journey—getting to the "right" plan was not the point. Participants took the game seriously, but not literally. Even though each Brother in the room could easily identify himself and his school on the game board, the Brothers didn't waste time protecting their turf. After all, it was "just a game."

What's more, says Brother David, "The combination of the documentary film and the board game really helped us to start facing the stark reality of the future. The movie—difficult as it was—engaged the group's emotions. But then the game really excited them. The whole session was a catalyst for the actions that followed."

While the game would probably have worked without showing the film the night before, it wouldn't have been the same. The movie created an emotional tension that was then looking for release—which came with the outburst of positive energy during the board game.

Was all this design work necessary? What if the project team had taken a more typical approach and delivered detailed reports on the District's resources, with specific recommendations? "That would have just felt like more of the same," says Brother Ambrose. "I can't see how that would have had much impact."

In the months after the session, District leaders took the movie and board game on the road to regional sessions that engaged almost all Brothers across the three countries. They kicked off an ongoing strategy and planning process that's still paying dividends to this day—with surprising results.

While the Brothers' discussion in 2002 focused mainly on options for consolidating their operations, the scale and scope of the District's work has actually expanded since then. The District grew its impact by embracing a shift to lay leadership—to a greater degree than the Brothers had once thought possible. Today, lay teachers and administrators are stepping into the leadership roles vacated by retiring Brothers at different schools. The District has invested in extensive training and leadership-development programs to ensure that lay leaders are carrying forward the legacy and mission of the order.

"Our mission is as strong as it's ever been today—and probably stronger," says Brother David. The Narooma session alone could never have accomplished this result—but it's proved to be a critical catalyst. "If we hadn't had this process to help start us down the path, I really wonder where we would be today." [12]

<h2 style="text-align:center">KEY PRACTICE 3
CREATE A NARRATIVE ARC</h2>

At first glance, setting the agenda for a strategic conversation is essentially the same as for a standard meeting. In both cases, you need to generate a list of topics and activities, then sort them into a logical sequence that fits into the allotted time.

However, black belt designers approach their agendas with a different mind-set—even if the final result may appear similar on paper. They think in terms of creating a "narrative arc"—a flow of activities that moves from beginning to end, just like a good story line.

The narrative arc concept comes from the world of drama. The diagram below shows a classic dramatic arc, as described by the German playwright

Gustav Freytag in the mid-nineteenth century. This five-part structure—introduction of characters, rising action, climax, falling action, and resolution—captures the arc of most plays.[13]

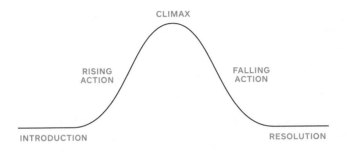

RISING
ACTION

FALLING
ACTION

INTRODUCTION

RESOLUTION

FREYTAG'S MODEL OF DRAMATIC ARC

Other genres have their own arcs. Syd Field's book *Screenplay* lays out the basic formula of most Hollywood movies.[14] Nancy Duarte's book *Resonate* reveals a basic structure that's common to many great speeches.[15] Many arcs are intuitive, following general principles but no set formula. Musical performers or deejays create set lists—sequences of songs—that explore different moods and paces, creating and releasing tension in ways that build over time. It's how Bruce Springsteen leaves his fans always wanting more, even at marathon shows lasting more than three hours.

What these approaches have in common—from drama to movies to speeches to concerts—is that they all focus on the experience from the participant's point of view. When you watch a Steven Spielberg movie, you see how much thought went into the pacing, the sequencing, and the overall building up of the experience. This approach is the opposite of that taken in most business presentations, where speakers "push" information based on the logic of their own thoughts, rather than the experience of their audience.

Given that strategic conversations are more fluid than a play or a movie—participants have more say in where the story goes—black belt designers don't follow a set formula in crafting their arcs. Rather, they customize the experience based on an understanding of the specific group of people and the issues they're facing.

To make this concrete, consider two different ways of thinking about the agenda and narrative arc of the Christian Brothers' strategic conversation. The diagram opposite shows what an agenda might have looked like if the team had taken a standard meeting approach.

This agenda makes perfect sense and might even get to decent results. By the end of the two days, with good facilitation support, the group should have a handle on the nature and extent of the challenge, plus an initial road map for making some progress. But this approach has one problem: it's bloodless. It asks the group to tackle the District's challenge as if it were a complex math problem—not a human challenge with implications for every participant plus the thousands of kids counting on the Brothers for an education.

By contrast, the actual session agenda included many of the above elements—but focused much more on the emotional and psychological journey of participants. The diagram on page 136 shows the agenda from the session, expressed as an arc experienced by the group.

As we mentioned, the big surprise of this session was how much fun the Demography in Action game proved to be—even though the Brothers were taking a hard and practical look at their own decline. Part of this effect was due to the playful nature of the game board itself and the way that the activity was set up. But just as important was that the group had already hit rock bottom the night before, in watching the emotional video about the demise of the order of nuns. Because they'd already had their cathartic moment imagining the worst-case outcome, they were now freed up emotionally to tackle the challenges of their own future with greater clarity and courage— and even humor.

The most important point about creating a narrative arc is this: it's hard—if not impossible—for a strategic conversation to generate insight and impact unless there are emotionally challenging moments. While it would be great to design a session that starts with an emotional high point

DRAFT AGENDA
FOR STRATEGIC CONVERSATION
WITH THE CHRISTIAN BROTHERS

DAY ONE: CURRENT ASSESSMENT   DAY TWO FUTURE PLANNING

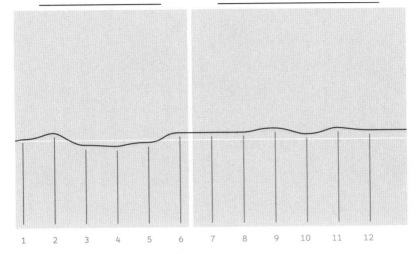

1   Welcome and introductions

2   Objectives and agenda

3   Overview of District operations
    Educational outcomes, financials, and
    human resources

4   Gap analysis
    10-year demographic and financial
    projections for District

5   Portfolio analysis
    Drill down on current operations and
    projections by school

6   Synthesis
    "Bucket" schools into major categories
    (strong, stable, at risk)

7   Brief review of Day One outcomes

8   Brainstorm options for strengthening
    "stable" and "at risk" schools

9   Breakout activity
    Create draft of 10-year plan for
    District improvement
    (four small groups)

10 Report-out of draft 10-year plans
    for District

11 Synthesis
    Identify major areas of agreement and
    divergence across plans

12 Next steps
    Commitments to continued progress

NARRATIVE ARC OF THE STRATEGIC CONVERSATION
WITH THE CHRISTIAN BROTHERS

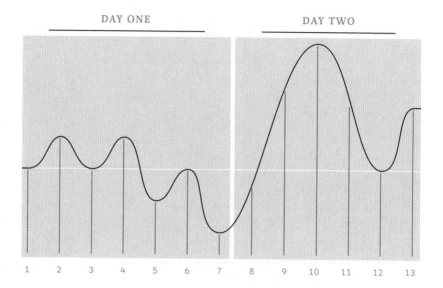

DAY ONE   DAY TWO

1   Workshop objectives and agenda

2   Opening remarks from leadership
     raising urgency and posing the
     challenge

3   Initial discussion on developing a
     vision for the District to 2010

4   Interview feedback and discussion
     Agree on key areas of alignment

5   Interview feedback and discussions
     Prioritize key issues for resolution

6   Dinner break

7   Viewing of documentary film on the
     closing of an order of nuns in US

8   Debrief of video
     Reflections on the challenge

9   Review of pre-readings on orders
     that have successfully addressed the
     challenges of decline

10   Future simulations
     "Demography in Action" board game in
     small groups

11   Report out from simulation exercise
     and plenary discussion

12   Key agreements on path forward

13   Leadership commitment to carry
     process forward

and just keeps getting higher, we've never seen or heard of any. At every successful strategic conversation we've been a part of, there is at least one moment where the group feels the burn of real tension. By contrast, most standard meetings tend to start in a neutral emotional gear and stay there throughout. No wonder they leave so few traces afterward.

The next time you approach an agenda for a strategic conversation, try thinking less like an air traffic controller juggling a list of topics and interests—and more like a screenwriter or deejay.

MEMORABLE EXPERIENCES CAN TRIGGER THE DESIRE TO ACT

Strategic conversations that follow the three key practices above—promoting active learning, engaging participants as whole people, and following a narrative arc—can become memorable experiences. Participants at these sessions can usually recall their main points, sometimes decades later. These vivid experiences are encoded firmly in their brains; the memories would be hard to get rid of even if they wanted to.

But being memorable for its own sake isn't the point. If it were, fun gimmicks could also do the trick, such as a massive fireworks display or the surprise appearance of a celebrity with no relevance to the program. While the two stories in this chapter are elaborate examples of powerful experiences, you can create them with far less time and far fewer resources. Recall that Neil Grimmer's Baby Food Fight took just two hours out of a board meeting, with minimal prep work.

In a provocative article titled "Strategy as Experienced," Professor Jeanne Liedtka of the University of Virginia's Darden School of Business gives her explanation for why so many strategy processes have so little impact. The problem, she writes, is that "nobody really cares about these strategies. Leaders must move beyond incorporating solid strategic thinking and effective communication in order to succeed: strategies must be *felt* as personally meaningful and compelling by the members of the organization who must adopt new behaviors in order to execute them. And thinking alone won't get you there." [16]

Liedtka distinguishes between what she calls *strategy as thought* versus *strategy as experienced*—both of which are necessary. The purpose of the former is to produce clear goals that a group of people can work toward. The purpose of the latter is to generate shared desires. "Desire, not goal-directedness," she writes, "is the true driver of behavioral change."

Once a group has the desire to do something, setting goals is much more straightforward. But clear goals without desire behind them will fail to motivate. What made the strategic conversations at Intuit and the Christian Brothers so effective is that participants in both cases *felt* the need for change in a way that rarely happens in a standard meeting. After both sessions, it was hard to imagine participants going back to their "real" work and ignoring the agreements they'd come to together.

You could argue that both outcomes were inevitable. Intuit had no choice but to get behind mobile—that's where their customers were heading. And the Christian Brothers had to deal with their aging challenge sooner rather than later if they wanted their important mission of educating kids to thrive. Yet, as we'll discuss in the next chapter, organizations routinely ignore obvious facts—sometimes to the point of self-destruction.

As we've pointed out before, it's nearly impossible to solve an adaptive challenge in just one strategic conversation. But it is possible to design experiences that leave participants knowing and feeling that they must do something. In both of the cases in this chapter, it became clear that moving forward with the current strategies was not an option. When confronted with an adaptive challenge, mustering the collective courage to let go of the status quo can be the most important step of all.

CONFRONTING THE "YABBUTS"

Now that you're familiar with how to design strategic conversations—and have seen how they can lead to moments of impact—it's time to visit the dark side.

By this point, we suspect you've collected a good number of *yabbuts* in your head. That's the word that innovation-strategy pioneer Larry Keeley uses to describe thoughts like "*Yeah*, sure, this all sounds good—*but* here's why this would never work in my organization."

Well-designed strategic conversations typically deliver good results—but there are exceptions. Below are a few sessions that didn't make our list of success stories. (For obvious reasons, most of the situations described in this chapter are disguised.)

▸ *A consulting team spent weeks preparing for a strategy session with the leaders of a large manufacturing company to consider different global expansion options. The day before the session, the team was surprised to learn that the company's chairman—who was not slated to attend—would be swinging by sometime during the session to announce the company's new growth strategy. Sure enough, late in the afternoon, the chairman popped in, tossed the consultants out of the room, and gave the leaders their marching orders—turning the event into a useless sideshow.*

▸ *A highly profitable consumer technology business was under serious attack from a disruptive new technology. Its leaders assembled a team of experts in technology, consumer trends, and new business models to help them explore innovation options. During the second day of the session, the unit president started ducking out of the room—a luxury skybox at a baseball stadium—to prepare for a tough earnings call.*

At the end of the session, as the experts were presenting their most promising ideas, the president dashed back in the room and let fly a tirade that lay waste to all their hard work: "Dammit, none of these ideas are going to help us meet our numbers next quarter! Don't you understand? Big companies don't innovate! Small companies innovate—and we buy them! What should we be buying— and now?" The business collapsed over the next few years, and the president is long gone.

▸ *In 2008, just months before the global financial crisis hit, leaders of a big insurance company gathered to contemplate the business implications of four different scenarios on the future of the global economy. Three of the scenarios were relatively upbeat, but the last one—titled "Meltdown!"—featured a US-led global financial crisis. When discussion came around to this story, some of the most senior executives rejected it because, if true, it would make the firm's near-term financial goals unreachable. After heated debate, the group declared the scenario impossible and refused to engage with it. In the months that followed, they watched helplessly as this "impossible" scenario played out in reality, wreaking havoc on their business.*

Although teams can spend a lot of time worrying about such epic disasters as these, they're exceedingly rare; we haven't met a black belt who can recall more than one or two. Instead, strategic conversations tend to get undermined in ways that are far more mundane and subtle—yet just as dangerous.

We've studied all the "moments of nonimpact" we could find and uncovered a few clear patterns. Most of the time, when a session flops, it's because it fell victim to at least one of three big yabbuts: politics, near-termism, and what we call the *karaoke curse*. While the yabbuts exist as background noise in all organizations, strategic conversations tend to bring them into the foreground. Any one of them can cause a session to flounder. Together, they can create a system of resistance that can feel impossible to cut through.

If the preceding chapters were about teaching you the tools of the trade, then this chapter is about suiting you up for battle. If your next session is going to be worth the time, effort, and expense that goes into it, you'll have to confront the yabbuts head-on.

YABBUT 1
POLITICS

If you think your office politics are tricky, you should try hanging out with chimpanzees.

Dutch primatologist Frans de Waal and his colleagues spent a few thousand hours with a colony of chimps at Burgers' Zoo in Arnhem, Netherlands. His classic book *Chimpanzee Politics: Power and Sex among Apes*—first published in 1982—is an enthralling account of chimpanzee society that reveals a lot about our human workplaces.[1]

Our closest living evolutionary relatives—who share at least 95 percent of our DNA—can be surprisingly skillful politicians. The chimps in de Waal's book are constantly jockeying for position and "sucking up" to their superiors. They trade favors with allies and build complex coalitions that shift over time. When chimps become aggressive, they're careful to accomplish their goals without going over the edge. Once in a while, they lead dramatic coups that reset the balance of power.

De Waal and his crew staged a few well-chosen experiments that revealed just how subtle and advanced the chimps' political skills were. Once, when the fiercest alpha male (named Yeroen) was huddled near his two major rivals, the researchers introduced a fresh supply of special food just to see what would happen.

A short while ago, we threw a large amount of oak leaves out of our observation window. Seeing that Yeroen was approaching at full speed, bluffing as he came, none of the other apes dared to go near the leaves. Yeroen gathered up the whole pile, but ten minutes later each member of the group, from large to small, had a share of the booty. For the adult male, the amount that he himself possesses is not important. What matters is who does the distributing among the group.[2]

This scene reveals a sophistication of intent and planning that we don't normally associate with animals. De Waal makes it clear that Yeroen was risking serious physical injury—the other two alpha males could easily have taken him on. Yeroen took this risk not to eat the leaves himself, but to shore up his position with the group.

The next time you find yourself in a budget battle where leaders are protecting "their" people, keep in mind that we didn't invent the game of politics. It's hardwired into our DNA. Yet, with rare exception, people talk about politics as something that other people do. When was the last time you heard someone say, "I'm playing politics here"? In most places, it's fine to say to a coworker, "I'd really like to make more money." But admitting that you're seeking power for yourself is one of the biggest taboos of organizational life.

The phrase *political organization* is redundant; all organizations are political. Every participant at a strategic conversation brings self-interest to the table, even if few of them will talk about it freely. If you read de Waal's book, you'll find that monkey business easily explains half or more of the political behavior in human organizations. If you read Machiavelli's *Prince*— completed in 1513—its nuanced counsel on the various means for gaining, yielding, and retaining power will fill in a good bit more of the picture.

ORG CHARTS ARE A HOAX

If you've studied primate behavior, Machiavelli, and the classic drama of the Greeks and Shakespeare, you've got most of what there is to know about modern office politics. If you want more nuance, we suggest reading Art Kleiner's *Who Really Matters: The Core Group Theory of Power, Privilege, and Success*—a tour-de-force analysis of how organizational politics works.[3] Kleiner's book delivers two main takeaways for strategic conversations.

First, leadership teams don't make the big decisions. At the top of every organization—and many units—sits a group called the executive committee or leadership team. But these teams are rarely decision-making bodies, though they often pose as such. Rather, they exist so that people who head up these various units and functions can coordinate their activities—a worthwhile but different purpose.

Kleiner shows that in most organizations it's an informal subset of leaders—what he calls the *core group*—that makes the real decisions. Leadership team members who aren't in the core group—such as the head of IT or a smaller business unit—have limited access to the real machinations of power. At most leadership-team decision-making meetings about big strategic issues, core group members share their decisions with everyone else, often in the guise of open dialogue.

This observation is important because it explains the fog of mystery that can shroud organizational politics and float into strategic conversations. Just as most of the action in the US Congress happens offstage and not on C-SPAN, the real debate over high-stakes issues in most organizations often takes place outside of formal meetings and events.[4]

The second big insight from Kleiner's book is that, while there's no such thing as "no politics," there is a continuum that runs from "bad" to "good." Bad politics is about individual self-interest, control over resources, and empire building. Gaining and retaining power—and enjoying its many perks—is its own end. Good politics, by contrast, involves honest debate about ideas, values, and an organization's future direction.

It's usually easy to tell whether an organization tilts toward good politics or bad. When you interview executives at an organization where bad politics rules, their comments tend to feature elaborate rationales for why their unit, department, or team is doing well, while all problems lie elsewhere. They can't stop posturing and positioning.

By contrast, when you interview executives at a place where good politics dominates, their comments are focused on big-picture issues—what customers are saying, which trends are driving change in their markets, and so on. When they talk about internal issues, it's more in the spirit of trying to understand complex personalities and group dynamics rather than gaming them.

To be sure, there are many shades of gray in between. Most people will enter a strategic conversation with mixed motives. Even "good" politicians must work to gain and retain power in order to be effective. The key is to

COMMON POLITICAL PITFALLS

Sometimes, bad politics can blow up a session. In *Learnings from the Long View*, futurist Peter Schwartz recalls a situation where a CEO called for a supposedly open dialogue about future directions for the company—just so he could flush out and expel all executives whose ideas differed from his own. (Schwartz fired the client afterward.)[5]

More often, though, bad politics will undermine strategic conversations in more insidious ways. Below is a list of common political pitfalls that exist in all organizations. When one starts to dominate your strategic conversation, you can be sure that bad politics is taking charge.

▸ *Unclear decision rights.* It's remarkable how many leaders refuse to declare openly who will make the ultimate decisions—even when it's obvious. Most people can handle not having the final say so long as they feel the process is open and legitimate. When decision rights are left vague, participants often start acting as if they were in a decision-making session, making matters messy.

▸ *Fake participation.* Senior executives sometimes call for strategic conversations when they have little or no interest in hearing divergent opinions—or, worse, when they want to ram through their own program while making it look as if the idea came from a group. But most people have strong BS detectors. We know when we're being humored instead of heard and can be quick to disengage or otherwise undermine such proceedings.

- *Border policing.* Every organization struggles—to some degree—with the "silo problem," or subgroups within the organization seeing their self-interest and identity in opposition to other subgroups or even the organization as a whole. Sometimes these silos become so walled off that constructive dialogue or collaboration between subgroups becomes nearly impossible.

- *Excessive deference.* Naturally people will pay close attention to the opinions and behavior of a strategic conversation's senior participants. However, this can make a group reluctant to challenge truly dreadful ideas posed by senior leaders.

- *Undiscussable elephants in the room.* Every organization has issues that can be tough to talk about openly in a group setting. Sometimes this awkwardness becomes an outright taboo on certain topics or words. If one of these issues is raised in a strategic conversation, it can shut down dialogue fast.

- *Agenda hijacks.* By contrast, some issues can become *too* discussable, taking up far more time and energy than they merit. This often happens when a participant hijacks the agenda by trying to push through a pet idea or project that's only loosely related to the session's objectives.

- *Shifting the burden.* In one strategic conversation with a financial services company, a business unit head took a lot of flack for his unit's sharp decline in revenues—despite the fact that sales in his channel had crashed industrywide. The leadership team refused to see the challenge as an external force that they needed to wrestle with together. Instead, they repeatedly referred to the revenue crash as "Hank's problem"—on the assumption that shaming him would somehow make him more "accountable."

- *Opting out.* This is probably the most common pitfall. Some or many participants decide that they have more to lose than gain by being honest about their opinions, so they hold back, hurting the quality of the dialogue.

keep a watchful eye out for common political pitfalls and address them in ways that can steer a strategic conversation away from bad politics and toward the good.

YABBUT 2
NEAR-TERMISM

Remember MySpace? In 2006, the popular social networking site was an online behemoth, with more visitors than Google. Until 2009, it was neck and neck with Facebook in a race to become the planet's dominant social media platform. But when MySpace and Facebook started pursuing sharply different growth strategies, their paths split—for good.

Facebook's strategy was to invest in new ways to delight its users; its teams spent a ton of time studying social networking behavior and using that data to anticipate—and create—what Facebookers would want next. MySpace chose to focus on near-term metrics such as page views and revenue targets in order to shore up the company's stock price. While Facebook kept rolling out new user-friendly features, inspiring members to join by the millions, MySpace's pages grew so busy with ads that its once-loyal users started flocking elsewhere.[6]

In 2011, News Corp. sold MySpace for just $35 million—a sharp discount from its purchase price of $580 million in 2005. The following year, Facebook went public, having reached a billion users globally and annual revenues of nearly $4 billion.[7]

MySpace is hardly the first or the last company to learn that a close-in focus can shortchange the future. In today's rapidly changing environment, all organizations need to balance short-term goals with long-term growth if they want to thrive beyond the next few quarters. Yet only a handful of innovative organizations are true masters at this balancing act.

In his book *Saving Capitalism from Near-Termism*, veteran Wall Street observer Alfred Rappaport lays out this problem in depressing detail.[8] The stock market used to be a place where regular people built their wealth. As recently as the mid-1980s, most shares in publicly traded stocks were sold to individual investors who would buy and hold them for growth. Today, the market's a place where traders (and computers) speculate for a quick buck. Most shares are bought by institutional investors—pension funds or mutual fund managers—who keep them for a year, on average, before trading them again. Meanwhile, Rappaport notes, CEOs and other executives are coming and going faster than ever—so much so that they can seem more like highly paid contractors than stewards of their organizations.

This short-term bias cascades down an organization. While leaders give lofty speeches about visions for the future, the metrics they create and enforce tell people what really matters: near-term performance. As a result, work today can feel like an endless race around a Formula One track with blinders on—a race that's always getting faster thanks to technologies that enable 24-7 "always on" reaction time across the globe. But driving on the same road—around and around, faster and faster—gets you only so far.

"We've misinterpreted this whole competing-on-speed thing in business today," says Peter Johnson, the longtime head of strategy for pharmaceutical maker Eli Lilly and Company. "The fact is, when things are happening very fast, it's even *more* important that we stop and take the time to think deeply."[9] When you're taking sharp curves at a hundred miles per hour, mistakes are far more likely to be fatal. The highway of business is littered with the wrecks of firms (and people) that ran themselves into the ground while producing solid quarterly results.

Unfortunately, near-termism is hardwired in our brains. One of the best-documented cognitive biases is temporal discounting—that people predictably put a higher value on benefits or costs that are in their face now over ones that will come later. Temporal discounting is a big part of the reason we fail to exercise, succumb to tempting foods, "forget" to floss our teeth, neglect to save for retirement, or suffer from disabling addictions.

In the famous Stanford Marshmallow Experiment, researchers found that the ability of children to delay gratification by choosing to take two marshmallows in twenty minutes rather than one marshmallow now had long-term predictive value. In follow-up studies, preschoolers who were able to wait the extra time had greater self-control and success as adults.[10] Organizations could learn a lot from these kids. We need more incentives to offset the powerful effects of temporal discounting—not reinforce it—if we want to thrive for years to come.

By definition, strategic conversations deal with the most important issues facing an organization. Yet it's often astonishing how many participants will do everything they can to steer the conversation back to the more comfortable terrain of in-your-face problems and quick fixes. Sometimes, it feels as if you can actually see the urgent chasing the important out of the room, as people frantically duck out to deal with calls and e-mails.

YABBUT 3
THE KARAOKE CURSE

Ever been to a karaoke bar? After a couple of drinks, even a midlevel marketing manager might believe he can belt out Sinatra's "My Way" as well as the chairman of the board. After all, it *looks* easy when other people sing well. Reality shows such as *American Idol* tap into the fantasy that the average person, with a bit of practice, can transform into the next superstar.

Alas, talent doesn't work that way. While we all have more natural aptitude for some things than for others, raw talent doesn't amount to much without a lot of effort. Books by Malcolm Gladwell (*Outliers*) and Geoff Colvin (*Talent Is Overrated*) show that—time after time—people who appear to have amazing "natural" talent turn out to have put in at least ten thousand hours of deliberate practice, such as Yo-Yo Ma, who started playing the cello at age four.[11]

Karaoke skills is our term for areas where people's confidence tends to exceed their competence. Driving is a classic karaoke skill: surveys show that a vast majority of people rate themselves "above average" as drivers. By contrast, a few things that are definitely *not* karaoke skills are brain surgery, nuclear physics, gymnastics, Chinese calligraphy, and firefighting. If you rarely or never do these things, you wouldn't kid yourself that you're good at them.[12]

Strategic conversations tend to surface a number of karaoke skills, such as presenting, group facilitation, or collaboration skills. But the most important is strategic thinking. Like any serious skill, strategic thinking takes time to master, and you can quickly spot a black belt (or a karaoke performer) when you see one in action.

In recent years, Ellen Goldman has been conducting research on how executives develop strategic thinking skills. A former consultant who teaches at George Washington University, Goldman has led or been part of hundreds of strategic conversations over three decades. While most of her work has been with health-care delivery organizations, her interviews with CEOs and extensive surveys have broad relevance.

"In my dissertation research," Goldman says, "most of the CEOs that I interviewed said things like 'I just assumed that when I was made CEO, I would think the way I had to think.'" These CEOs knew they needed to upgrade their communication skills or financial acumen, but not one of them saw strategic thinking as a priority before taking the job. "Person after person in my interviews said, 'I've never really thought about that before.'"[13]

Most executives reach their positions by excelling at their day job of operations and execution—not by exercising their strategic thinking skills. But once they assume leadership roles, strategic thinking *is* their day job. Goldman found that developing strategic thinking requires a long period of deliberate practice—usually a decade or more, at increasing levels of complexity. She identifies nine types of experiences that are important to becoming a better strategic thinker, including leading a major growth initiative, managing a serious crisis, and being mentored by someone with strong strategic thinking skills.[14]

Most organizations don't develop their leaders' skills in such a systematic way. Business school courses, outside the context of real work, can help only so much. As a result, even the leadership teams of huge organizations can have uneven capabilities when it comes to the key elements of strategic thinking.[15]

You don't need these skills to *participate* in a strategic conversation. Anyone with keen observations about his or her organization and its envi-

KEY ELEMENTS OF STRATEGIC THINKING

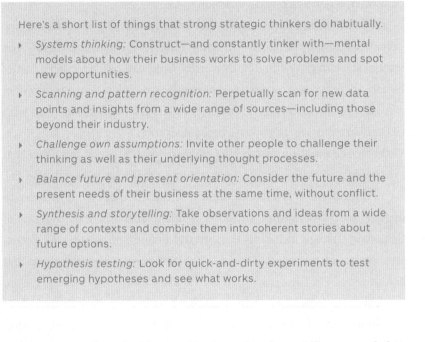

Here's a short list of things that strong strategic thinkers do habitually.

▸ *Systems thinking:* Construct—and constantly tinker with—mental models about how their business works to solve problems and spot new opportunities.

▸ *Scanning and pattern recognition:* Perpetually scan for new data points and insights from a wide range of sources—including those beyond their industry.

▸ *Challenge own assumptions:* Invite other people to challenge their thinking as well as their underlying thought processes.

▸ *Balance future and present orientation:* Consider the future and the present needs of their business at the same time, without conflict.

▸ *Synthesis and storytelling:* Take observations and ideas from a wide range of contexts and combine them into coherent stories about future options.

▸ *Hypothesis testing:* Look for quick-and-dirty experiments to test emerging hypotheses and see what works.

ronment can make valuable contributions. But these skills are needed to effectively *lead* a strategic conversation—to guide it toward meaningful insights and outcomes. While that leadership can come from anyone, strategic conversations tend to work best when the people in senior roles bring strong strategic thinking skills into the room.

Leaders are often so focused on answers that they have little patience for strategic conversations. At one strategic conversation with a technology company, the CEO brought work to a screeching halt with this frustrated outburst: "I don't see why you're making this all so complicated. We just need to create products and services that people want, at a price that they're willing to pay. What's so hard about that?" After this bit of karaoke, you could practically see the beads of sweat collecting on the forehead of the VP of strategy.

Leaders with underdeveloped strategic thinking skills often try to "fix" adaptive challenges with the same tools they use for technical challenges.

If you've got a hammer, as the saying goes, every problem looks like a nail. Faced with a mysterious decline in revenues or a surprising new competitor, such leaders will often grab the most comfortable hammer at hand—be it a reorganization, an acquisition, or a "strategic" plan to keep doing more of the same, just better.

CONFRONTING THE YABBUTS AS A SYSTEM OF RESISTANCE

Most of the time, the three yabbuts—politics, near-termism, and the karaoke curse—are manageable nuisances. Other times, they gang up to make a real mess.

Consider how the yabbuts can conspire within one person. Imagine a senior executive whose buy-in you need but who's not strong at strategic thinking. Odds are, he's going to feel uncomfortable confronting uncertainty and ambiguity for a day or two. If his peers show better strategic thinking skills in the session, this may make him anxious and trigger his political instincts. When that happens, he may dismiss the longer-term challenges and steer the discussion back to daily operational challenges, where he excels. Voilà! One person = three yabbuts.

This dynamic—a self-reinforcing feedback loop—can also play out across an organization. Most organizations are split into units that are tracked by their results and compete with one another for resources. At any moment, some units are doing better than others. Struggling units typically feel pressure to catch up to the others, which leads them to focus even more on the near term, cutting off attention and resources for longer-term issues.

Normally, this dynamic creates background noise—not pleasant, but hardly fatal. But when the organization faces an adaptive challenge, the yabbuts can turn up the volume. Focus on near-term performance intensifies, finger-pointing gets more heated, and developmental activities languish. As each yabbut gets louder, it amplifies the others.

Over time, if the yabbuts aren't addressed, the organization's focus becomes increasingly narrow and insular. Leaders spend their time worried about quarterly results and internal politics. Eventually, the failure to develop new offerings or capabilities erodes performance. As performance weakens, so does the capacity to develop successful strategies. The yabbuts are now working together in full force, and the organization is less able to deal with the adaptive challenge.

The resulting "doom loop" can play out over months or decades, depending on the pace of change in the organization and its markets. But whenever an organization allows the yabbuts to grow unchecked in the face of a serious adaptive challenge, the ultimate outcome is always the same.

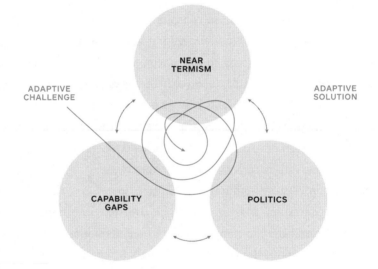

THE YABBUT DOOM LOOP

THE DOOM LOOP AT ENCYCLOPAEDIA BRITANNICA

For more than two centuries, *Encyclopaedia Britannica* was the ultimate reference authority in the English language. Launched in 1768, it could be found in the home libraries of George Washington and Thomas Jefferson. Albert Einstein, Charles Darwin, and John F. Kennedy were among its contributors. For decades, an army of salespeople marched door-to-door, impressing on parents the importance of the thirty-volume set to their children's education. Today, it's hard to imagine shelling out $1,500 to $2,000 to fill your living room with precious bound volumes. But up through the 1980s, *Encyclopaedia Britannica* was commonplace in the homes of educated Americans.

In 1985, Microsoft—then still an upstart company—invited Britannica to partner in creating a digital encyclopedia. Bill Gates thought that a digital edition of the popular reference could help drive growth of the budding home market for PCs. But Britannica, not wanting to cheapen its core product, rebuffed Gates's offer, choosing to chart its own path into the digital age.

In the following years, Britannica ran well ahead of the curve in experimenting with new media formats. It came out with the first multimedia encyclopedia on CD-ROM in 1989, when just 15 percent of American homes had a computer. In September 1994 it launched Britannica Online 1.0—months before the release of the pioneer web browser Netscape 1.0.

In 1993, Microsoft launched its own encyclopedia on CD-ROM, named *Encarta*—four years after Britannica's. While not as complete or authoritative, *Encarta* sold for just $99. Microsoft was able to charge so little for *Encarta* because its objective was to grow the home market for PCs using the Microsoft operating system—not to become a book publisher.

A classic "disruptive innovation," *Encarta* proved good enough for many buyers. In its first year, Microsoft sold about 350,000 copies—three times Britannica's sales. In its second year, sales of *Encarta* tripled to more than a million. As Gates had hoped, *Encarta* helped to grow the market for PCs, which in turn grew the market for *Encarta*, creating a positive upward spiral.

Although most of *Encarta*'s sales were to first-time encyclopedia buyers, its arrival in the market hit Britannica hard. Sales of the company's prestigious print edition tumbled from 117,000 copies in 1993 to just 55,000 in 1996.

Meanwhile, Britannica made serious missteps in bringing its own digital encyclopedia to market. The company had released its first multimedia product in 1989—a multimedia version of *Compton's Encyclopaedia*, Britannica's down-market brand for grade-school kids. In doing so, it chose an off-putting pricing strategy. Buyers were offered a choice: they could get the digital edition free with purchase of a full set of the regular books—which made it seem cheap—or pay $895 for it. Not surprisingly, few did.

In 1994, faced with plummeting print sales, the company released a digital edition of the full *Encyclopaedia Britannica*, drawing on the power of its flagship brand. But it chose the same failed pricing model—and cranked it up a notch. This time, buyers could get the digital edition free with the purchase of the print books or pay a whopping $1,200 for the CDs alone. Again, buyers largely ignored it.

What happened? Britannica had a much better product than the competition's and was at one point ahead of the curve in exploring new media. Why did the company make such dubious choices? Strategic meltdowns such as the one Britannica experienced have many contributing factors—but some combination of the yabbuts is usually present. At Britannica, they could be found most easily among the company's sales force.

In the early 1990s, Britannica employed more than two thousand salespeople, who drove the bulk of its revenues and enjoyed high pay and political power. In hindsight, it seems obvious that Britannica's best hope was to migrate to a new model where it sold a much larger volume of digital products at a much lower price. But the sales force wasn't interested in new models that could threaten their standard commission of $500 to $600 per set. Britannica's leadership couldn't find a new model that would work for both customers and their powerful sales force. As a result, most of the latter eventually lost their jobs.

Britannica's leaders saw the digital age coming from far away—and yet it still hit hard when it came. In 1990, the company enjoyed record-high sales and revenues. By 1996, when sales and revenues had collapsed by half, it was sold to Jacob Safra, a Lebanese financier, in a fire sale for just $135 million (roughly a third of that year's revenues). In the ensuing years, as the new ownership struggled to restore Britannica to its former glory, Google and Wikipedia piled on to the challenges started by the PC and *Encarta*. In

2012, Britannica announced it would stop printing books entirely. Today, it soldiers on as a faint, online shadow of its former glory.[16]

CLUELESSNESS IS NOT THE PROBLEM

In Gabriel García Márquez's novella *Chronicle of a Death Foretold*, almost everyone in town knows that the Vicario brothers are going to kill Santiago Nasar for tarnishing their sister's reputation. The brothers boast about their plan to anyone who will listen. While almost nobody wants the murder to happen, and it's not clear that the brothers mean to go through with their plan, this slow-motion tragedy winds its way forward with grim inevitability. When the brothers finally shoot Nasar, it's anticlimactic. Afterward, everybody wonders why nobody stopped it.[17]

Most of the time, not only do leaders of floundering organizations see the bullet coming—they can't stop talking about it. They sit through endless presentations on the bullet's velocity, force, and trajectory. As it gets closer, bullet initiatives and shield task forces pop up all over the place. By the time the bullet arrives, everyone knows all about it—so much so that they're bored of the topic. Yet, they let it hit them anyway.

The story of Britannica's fall is iconic because—like the townsfolk in Márquez's novella—its leaders saw the bullet coming from far away. They were tracking the digital revolution closely and took early, meaningful steps in the right directions. It just wasn't enough to overcome the resistance of the sales force, who saw new media products as a threat to their immediate income. While we'll never know what kind of meetings they had at Britannica as things were heading south in the early 1990s, it's probably a safe guess that near-termism and politics played important roles in their outcome.

Look closely at any organization that's failed to seize an important opportunity or to respond to an adaptive challenge and you won't find a bunch of clueless people. More likely, you'll find good people struggling with too-timid experiments and unproductive strategic conversations. The pages of business history are full of stories about great companies that saw the future coming well in advance and let others lead the way. Kodak was experimenting with digital cameras in the mid-1970s, while Xerox PARC was developing several essential components of the modern PC; music companies could see the digital revolution coming and were experimenting with new offers, yet it was Apple—an industry outsider at the time—that seized the initiative.

Machiavelli nailed the core essence of this dynamic five hundred years ago, in this passage from *The Prince*:

> *Nothing is more difficult to handle, more doubtful of success, nor more danger-ous to manage, than to put oneself at the head of introducing new orders. For the introducer has all those who benefit from the old orders as enemies, and he has lukewarm defenders in all those who might benefit from the new orders. This lukewarmness arises partly from fear of adversaries . . . and partly from the incredulity of men.*[18]

The American novelist Upton Sinclair made the same observation, more succinctly: "It is difficult to get a man to understand something when his salary depends on him not understanding it."

We've been in many sessions with teams that are in the throes of a doom loop, and it can be a tough spiral to exit. You know you're in a strategic conversation where the yabbuts are in firm control when participants:

▸ *Use the phrase* if only *a lot. As in "If only Customer X would start buying the way they used to buy again." Or "If only we had ten percent more top-line revenue."*

▸ *Cherry-pick their data like crazy—clutching onto rare nuggets of informa-tion that support weak theories while explaining away a slew of inconvenient facts.*

▸ *Become increasingly insular and disconnected, ignoring voices of friendly dissent from within and excluding external experts from contributing their perspectives.*

▸ *Talk about the past more than the future and seem desperate to go back in time to some bygone era when business was good.*

▸ *Spend more time trying to figure out whom to blame and how to massage internal communications than how to solve problems.*

As an outsider, when you find yourself in a conversation like this, it can feel as if you were shipwrecked on the Island of Magical Thinking. While on the island, everything is logical and makes perfect sense. But the minute you step foot off the island and observe it from even a short distance, it looks ridiculous.

While each organization has its unique version of the yabbuts, they're all variations on a theme. The roots of adaptive failure lie deep in human nature. They start in our DNA and reptilian brain, where we're wired for fight or flight in a struggle over resources. They draw comfort from our cognitive biases that make us favor the present over the future and fear losses more than we seek gains. And they're fueled by our deep emotional connection to our past success. None of these forces are going away anytime soon.

VUCA WORLD DEMANDS BETTER STRATEGIC CONVERSATIONS

The forces of VUCA World—technology change, social change, globalization, and more—are shooting slow-motion bullets like buckshot across our economy. On the current watch list are huge pharmaceutical companies with their "blockbuster" drugs; publishing houses tied to declining retail channels and outdated pricing models; a host of technology companies tied to the PC computing platform; and big-box retailers of many stripes. These markets—among others—will look very different in five or ten years. If history is any guide, it won't be today's incumbents who lead the way.

The challenges of VUCA World don't only vex large, older companies. They can also be found in many cultural institutions—such as public libraries and museums—that struggle for relevance in a time of information overload and proliferating media choices. They can be found in our colleges and universities, as students and parents experiment with alternatives to high-cost schooling. And they can even be found in dynamic, younger companies once their initial rapid-growth phase slows down.

Adaptive failure carries huge costs for society. Workers and their families lose their livelihoods. Communities see their vital institutions diminish. Meanwhile, our society and policymakers struggle in vain to come to grips with "wicked" long-term challenges such as climate change, broken healthcare and education systems, and mounting public debt, among others.

At a time when we desperately need better strategic conversations, they're hard to come by. John Seely Brown—the bestselling author—has participated in scores of strategic conversations over the past four decades, as an executive, board member, and outside expert. Reflecting on his experiences, Brown says, "I don't believe that organizations can succeed today without good strategic conversations—and yet it's very seldom that I see them." [19]

While better conversations alone can't solve all our problems, it's hard to make real progress without them. Strategic conversations offer our best hope for flushing out and conquering the powerful yabbuts. They're a critical resource for resolving adaptive challenges.

And *that's* why we wrote this book.

MAKE *YOUR* MOMENT

A few years ago, *impact investing* was an obscure and little-used term. Today, it describes a multibillion-dollar global industry. Part of how it got there was one well-designed strategic conversation.

You may have heard of socially responsible investing. It's the practice of steering investment dollars away from companies and industries seen as harmful—such as those that have questionable environmental or labor practices—and toward those that are more socially or environmentally friendly.

Impact investing goes one step further. Investors place funds directly into projects that create value by addressing specific social challenges, such as an affordable-housing development that reinvigorates a blighted neighborhood while turning a profit or at least breaking even.

In 2007, leaders of the Rockefeller Foundation believed that this model of investing for social benefit was a great idea—and that it needed to scale faster. So they organized a gathering of a few dozen people who were leading scattered projects around the world. At this initial meeting, the group coalesced around the term *impact investing* to describe the field and agreed to keep working toward its advancement.

Bolstered by the success of that first meeting, Rockefeller decided to organize a second, more ambitious gathering, with a larger and more diverse group. In June 2008, forty-one participants headed to Northern Italy for a two-day strategic conversation on the future of impact investing. Rockefeller engaged Monitor Institute—a consulting team that designs strategic conversations for the social-benefit sector—to help with the session. Their approach closely followed the design we've laid out in this book.

"The idea was to put in the room people who were working on very similar things but who normally didn't talk to one another," says Antony Bugg-Levine, the project leader for the Rockefeller Foundation at the time. "We thought the development of impact investing could be accelerated if we brought together the leaders of the field for a few days of intense and focused collaboration."

Because participants were already well-versed in the issues, *the purpose* of the session was related to Shaping Choices. What could this group do to increase the amount of dollars invested for impact? How might they spread awareness of this investment option? While they went in with a few specific hypotheses of possible initiatives, they couldn't be sure which ideas participants would embrace and run with.

The Rockefeller and Monitor Institute team went to great lengths to *engage multiple perspectives*. They conducted more than fifty in-depth interviews with people working at the frontiers of the field to understand the full range of perspectives. In each interview they asked who was leading the way in different areas. They worked their networks hard until they had a complete picture of the landscape of actors. Then they assembled a dream team of impact investors that included investors from huge global banks and small local nonprofits and from Asia, Africa, North America, and South America. Investors focused on areas from agriculture to housing, from alternative energy to economic development. No group like this had ever before gathered.

By talking with participants in advance, the team developed a clear understanding of the key similarities and differences within this diverse group. They used this understanding to *frame the issues* in ways that would resonate with participants.

One frame was a simple two-by-two matrix that situated participants in terms of their relative focus on social benefit versus economic returns. This simple frame helped them talk about the different approaches they brought to the field—and how they related to one another. A second frame was a short list of six ways participants might help accelerate the field's development, distilled from the interviews. These were presented as ideas for the group to expand on, prioritize, and improve as they saw fit.

When trying to bring busy people together, it helps to invite them to a serene Italian retreat—the Rockefeller Foundation's Bellagio Center—in early summer. Against this backdrop, the team made additional efforts to *set the scene*, such as creating a large visual timeline that depicted the recent history of impact investing. As participants arrived at the meeting room, they were greeted by this colorful timeline of global trends, headline events, and images of work in the field—to which they were invited to add their own personal experiences and observations. Their handwriting gradually covered the timeline, creating a vivid sense that they were all part of a larger story.

Putting these pieces together, the team designed *an experience* to maximize impact under unusual circumstances. "It was a group of volunteers who didn't know each other well," says Katherine Fulton, head of Monitor Institute and lead facilitator at the session. "Since almost nobody was required to do anything after it was over, it was important that the conversation not only create new insights but also motivate people to act."

The team knew that, for anything to happen afterward, the group needed to build a sense of ownership for the ideas they were developing. So the team left ample time in the program for participants to work in self-organized groups around topics of their own choosing. Just as important, the team came to the session with the humility and courage to adapt the program in real time to the needs of the group.

Early on the second day, the team started to introduce additional content they'd brought to share. However, participants rebelled and made clear that they wanted to push harder on developing ideas they'd already come up with. "It was one of the scariest experiences I've had as a facilitator," Fulton says. "I remember looking around the room and not being sure if we could hold the group together at that point."

The team quickly rearranged the agenda to provide more time for breakout groups to dig deeper into specific areas for collaboration. By the end of the day, the group came to some shared insights. In particular, they agreed that the field, to grow more quickly, needed a formal structure for network building as well as more robust metrics and credentials.

As a direct result of the Bellagio session, several new projects were launched. The Global Impact Investing Network (GIIN) was established with Rockefeller Foundation support to raise awareness of the field and foster ongoing collaboration. GIIN also maintains a system of metrics (IRIS) to support and track progress in the field. In addition, the Global Impact Investing Ratings System (GIIRS) was founded to provide independent assessment of the social and environmental impact of companies and funds. Meanwhile, participants from the Bellagio session have helped grow the market by launching a number of new funds, some of them in collaboration.[1]

In just a few years, the field has gone from a cottage industry to a much more organized market. In a 2010 report, JP Morgan declared impact investing "an emerging asset class" with potential to reach $1 trillion in total investments by 2020.[2]

You can't credit one two-day event—no matter how great—for everything that happens afterward. Strategic conversations never "solve" big challenges in one fell swoop. But the Bellagio session was a moment of impact that created tremendous forward momentum.

"We were determined not to run this as a typical foundation meeting—and we didn't," says Bugg-Levine, who went on to become CEO of Nonprofit Finance Fund. "While foundation leaders live in a world of nuanced policy discussions and gradual consensus building, investors are more transaction oriented. That's why it was critical for this group to come to agreement around key insights quickly—and move on to action.

"The Bellagio session built our confidence to invest in field-building infrastructure, and many participants left with a stronger sense of belonging to a larger community and movement. Things have definitely happened faster as a result."[3]

DESIGNING STRATEGIC CONVERSATIONS AS MOMENTS OF IMPACT

You've seen how strategic conversations can help organizations resolve their toughest challenges. And you've seen how important it is to design strategic conversations rather than approach them as standard meetings. That's because successful strategies don't come from spreadsheets, slide shows, or detailed agendas.

Effective strategic choices come from great conversations where people combine their best ideas in new ways. They come from people sharing moments of insight so compelling they demand action. Such moments rarely show up without help. They happen when strategic conversations are designed, following the core principles we've outlined in this book. Of these principles, one looms largest.

Earlier we quoted Machiavelli on the hazards involved in "the introduction of a new order of things." Here's the rest of the quote:

Nothing is more difficult to handle, more doubtful of success, nor more dangerous to manage, than to put oneself at the head of introducing new orders. For the introducer has all those who benefit from the old orders as enemies, and he has lukewarm defenders in all those who might benefit from the new orders. This lukewarmness arises partly from fear of adversaries . . . and partly from the incredulity of men, who do not truly believe in new things unless they have come to have a firm experience of them [emphasis added].[4]

Machiavelli didn't design a lot of strategic conversations. But he realized that experience is not just the best teacher—it's the only one. When strategic conversations are designed as engaging experiences, people interact with issues in fundamentally different ways. They see them from the right distance—far enough away to have perspective yet close enough to also focus on the details that matter most. That's the space where new possibilities can take shape.

When a group enters this space, things can happen fast. Think about the five days that it took Gensler to help create a global workplace-design strategy. In setting up the session, it was tough to get approval for five days of time from a group of busy leaders from around the globe—it seemed an extravagance. Once in the room, that time flew by as the group was immersed in prototyping their future work environment. After the session, it was clear that those five days in person were far more productive than weeks or maybe even months of e-mails and conference calls.

Machiavelli was right. The best way to help people embrace any new idea is to give them a visceral experience of a future possibility. That's what creates a moment of impact.

LEADING STRATEGIC CONVERSATIONS THAT CREATE HOPE

In the last chapter, we talked about the yabbuts—the most common obstacles that stymie strategic conversations. We did this to make it clear that we understand what you're up against.

The yabbuts can be difficult to overcome, but in most situations they *can* be navigated by following the principles and practices we've laid out in this book. This entire book could be read as one big yabbut to the yabbuts.

Strategic conversations counteract the yabbuts. Defining a clear purpose and engaging multiple perspectives help to neutralize bad politics. Giving people a visceral experience of future possibilities keeps near-termism at bay. Framing the issues enables better strategic thinking and more creative solutions. In well-designed strategic conversations, the yabbuts don't disappear. But they get starved of oxygen long enough to get important work done.

That's when you—a budding black belt designer—can raise your ambition and lean in harder. Because your real goal is not just to neutralize the yabbuts. It's to get people focused on creating a better future with a sense of common purpose, in an environment where creativity and collaboration can flourish.

Just as the yabbuts can work as a self-reinforcing system (what we called the doom loop), well-designed strategic conversations can create a "hope loop." When a group takes on a forward-looking perspective, they're more likely to focus on their common interests. And when they focus on their common interests, they're more likely to help one another develop new strengths.

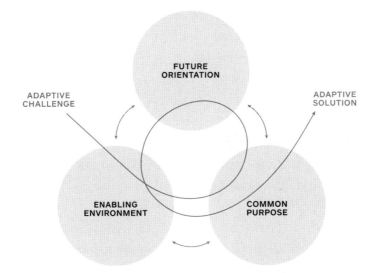

THE HOPE LOOP

Strategic conversations can set a hope loop like this in motion, creating the conditions for arriving at an adaptive solution. But it takes a bit more than a great experience design. It also takes leadership.

When the Christian Brothers confronted the depressing decline in their numbers, they could have quietly accepted their fate. Instead, they initiated a transition to lay leadership that's ensuring the future of their mission.

When mobile computing started taking off, Intuit could have held back—as many others did—to avoid internal squabbles over resources and ownership of the new platform. Instead, they focused on the future and got behind the emerging technology.

During a financial bubble, the leaders of Hagerty Insurance could have expanded recklessly in many directions at once. Instead they held firm, following the passions of their core audience of collectors—and were rewarded by the market even as other companies were hit hard.

None of these outcomes were inevitable. All of these organizations wrestle with the yabbuts. What makes them different is that they had the leadership to take on their challenges with courage and creativity. Ideally, this starts with the senior-most executives. But leadership can come from many people, including a strategic conversation's designer or facilitator, project team, and participants.

When leaders show the capacity to face an adaptive challenge, they can propel their organization forward in powerful ways. Confidence and optimism become contagious. People spend more of their time thinking about and planning great things they can do next. In our view, convening and designing great strategic conversations may just be the most important leadership skill you can have in VUCA World.

CREATIVE ADAPTATION BEATS CREATIVE DESTRUCTION

When adaptive challenges appear, many organizations waste time and energy trying to argue with the future. They deny facts and pine for the past. But sooner or later, the future wins.

We need less creative destruction in the world and a lot more *creative adaptation*—the ability of a person, an organization, or a society to evolve successfully into the future. This ability comes from strategic conversations. When things get complicated, there's no substitute for some good, old-fashioned thinking and talking.

The field of strategic conversations bears striking resemblance to the field of impact investing before the Bellagio session. Lots of dispersed activity and innovation are bubbling up from different places. Most black belt practitioners are aware of a few others like them—but not many. Plenty of good tools and practices are out there, but they haven't been brought together in one place. The community hasn't been convened or even identified so that fellow practitioners can help one another.

Our hope is that *Moments of Impact* will help unite and develop the field of strategic conversations, making the community of black belts more aware of itself—and enabling many others to develop this essential leadership skill.

STEPPING UP TO YOUR NEXT STRATEGIC CONVERSATION

We've argued that our approach to designing strategic conversations can lead to better results than standard strategy meetings. We also realize this approach is different from what people are used to and will thus feel risky to some. Yet the comfortable standard meeting approach carries a more likely risk: that the session will have little impact. When was the last time you can recall a linear-agenda, slideshow-driven meeting that drove real progress against a tough adaptive challenge?

It's unusual for people to walk away from a well-designed strategic conversation saying it was "okay." And it's rare for such sessions to fail. As you step up to designing your next strategic conversation, here are a few parting thoughts—from us and our chorus of black belts—on how to make it as successful as possible.

▸ Start with a "ripe" issue. *Effective strategic conversations focus on issues where the timing is right, when there's a sense of urgency—but not panic—to do something, either because of a growing threat or a growing opportunity that demands attention. Don't design a session for a topic that's too distant or too immediate in focus. These situations call for other approaches.*

▸ Fight for the time to do it right. *Tackling adaptive challenges takes time. But well-designed strategic conversations use that time efficiently. Two days of quality conversation among the right people can accomplish more than two months of unfocused effort. Don't let anyone persuade you to cram two days of work into two hours—it won't work, and it will just frustrate you and your participants.*

▸ Lead with empathy. *We can't emphasize this enough. You must take the time to understand participants' perspectives—their points of view—long before you walk into the room. Doing so will help you design a session that truly resonates with the group.*

▸ Put all the core principles to work. *The five principles and their key practices are a package deal, not an à la carte menu. If you set a fantastic scene but have the wrong purpose, it won't work. If you have the right perspectives in the room but the issues are poorly framed, it won't work. No single factor made the Bellagio session on impact investing successful—it was a combination of all five principles. The pieces all came together into something that was bigger and better than their sum.*

▸ Simplify, simplify, simplify. *Meeting organizers often try to cram too much material into too little time. Great design strives for simplicity, and great conversations need room to breathe. As you design your next session, resist the temptation to keep adding people in the room, topics to the agenda, and words on each slide. Find the courage to include only those elements that are essential to sparking a focused and productive strategic conversation.*

▸ Start small, then build. *If you're new to this approach, start with lower-stakes and less complex situations to build your skill and confidence—then expand from there. Find small ways to try this out with a friendly group before taking it into the boardroom.*

▸ Prep like hell—and then let go. *Black belts overprepare their sessions and then expect to improvise as events unfold in the room. This may sound like a contradiction, but it's not. People who are hyperprepared are much more comfortable and confident when they have to go off script.*

▸ No kamikaze missions! *Never lead a strategic conversation where the basic conditions for success aren't met—where the yabbuts are overpowering, the commitment to act isn't there, or the group refuses to take the time to do it right. If you run a mission that's doomed to fail, you'll damage the credibility of the approach—and may not get another chance.*

You can never wipe out risk entirely. Even in the best of circumstances, the yabbuts will conspire to make mischief. But most situations are not hopeless, just tricky. You don't need perfect conditions to lead a group into a moment of impact. You just need courage.

NO GOING BACK: THE COURAGE TO MAKE YOUR MOMENT

Each of the black belts we talked to in researching this book had his or her own story of developing from a novice to a master in this field. A common thread was that black belts didn't start out with the intent to become experts at designing strategic conversations. Rather, they found themselves leading strategic conversations by happenstance. Given an initial assignment, they made the effort to learn how to do it well. As their ability grew, so did their confidence and courage to be more ambitious. As they handled more complex and high-stakes situations successfully, they got hooked on the positive feedback they were getting and the impact they were having.

Several black belts spoke of their ability to design strategic conversations as a "secret weapon" in their career—an ability that helps them stand out and advance faster in their organizations. All of them agreed that, once you get the hang of this skill, there's no going back. Designing great strategic conversations is challenging and rewarding work that can also be fun. Most important, it's one way that just one person can have outsize impact on the future of an organization—and beyond.

So go ahead, make *your* moment. And when you do, don't be too surprised to find that you're pushing on an open door.

MOMENTS *of* IMPACT

STARTER KIT

TOOLS TO HELP YOU DESIGN
YOUR NEXT STRATEGIC CONVERSATION

Chris Ertel and Lisa Kay Solomon

DESIGNED BY MINE™

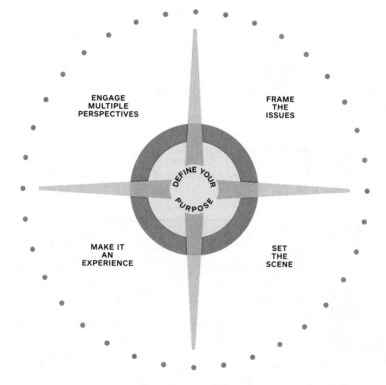

THE
STRATEGIC CONVERSATION
COMPASS

INTRODUCTION

Welcome to the *Moments of Impact* Starter Kit, a collection of tools and tips—based on the book—that will help you start designing strategic conversations.

Strategic conversations are creative and collaborative problem-solving sessions designed to address an adaptive challenge. Most organizational challenges are technical ones of applying established skills to well-defined problems, such as trying to find ways to raise revenues or cut costs by another 5 percent. Standard meetings work fine for these challenges. By contrast, adaptive challenges are messy, ambiguous, and open-ended. They require a different approach.

What adaptive challenge is your organization facing right now? The rise of a tough new competitor? The slow unraveling of a long-successful business model? The emergence of a disruptive new technology that presents both opportunities and threats? Surprising innovations coming from faraway markets?

In these volatile times, it would be odd if your organization weren't in the grips of at least one adaptive challenge. For a host of reasons, challenges like these are increasing in both frequency and intensity. Organizations have no choice but to deal with them head-on—or risk being left behind.

Superhero executives can't solve adaptive challenges by themselves. Addressing them requires collaboration from people with different perspectives from across the organization—and often beyond. And it requires an approach that's different from standard meetings and brainstorming sessions—our usual tools for collaboration.

Moments of Impact argues that strategic conversations are the best way to tackle adaptive challenges. But it's one thing to read about a process—and another to do it yourself. That's why we've included this Starter Kit.

Like the book, this kit is organized around five core principles. When you prepare for your next session, we suggest following them in the order shown in the diagram, keeping in mind that there will a fair amount of back-and-forth among the steps.

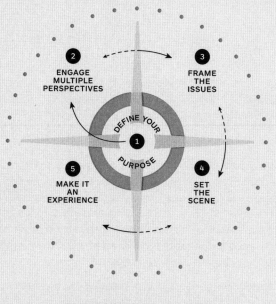

**THE CORE PRINCIPLES
AS PROCESS**

THREE WAYS TO USE THIS KIT

As a virtual coach

If you've got a big strategic conversation coming up and don't have time to read the whole book, you can quickly find many helpful ideas that will increase your odds of success. When you have time to read the book, you'll get a deeper understanding of the content and an intuitive feel for how to put these ideas into action.

As a checklist and handy reference

In *The Checklist Manifesto*, surgeon Atul Gawande makes the case that today's challenges are so complex that busy professionals can't possibly remember everything they know when they need it most. That's why pilots use checklists before they take off and doctors use them to improve the quality and consistency of health care. Even if you're a black belt at designing strategic conversations or have read this whole book, it can be hard to recall key points in the heat of the moment. We've put them together in one place, so you can scan them quickly and reabsorb their lessons.

As a shared playbook for teams

By providing a shared framework, process, and language, this kit will enable teams of people at different skill levels to design better strategic conversations—and to learn from one another along the way.

CORE PRINCIPLES
AND KEY PRACTICES

DEFINE YOUR PURPOSE
Seize your moment
Pick one purpose
Go slow to go fast

ENGAGE MULTIPLE PERSPECTIVES
Assemble a dream team
Create a common platform
Ignite a controlled burn

FRAME THE ISSUES
Stretch (don't break) mind-sets
Think inside *different* boxes
Choose a few key frames

SET THE SCENE
Make your space
Get visual
Do sweat the small stuff

MAKE IT AN EXPERIENCE
Discover, don't tell
Engage the whole person
Create a narrative arc

MAKING YOUR MOMENT: A KIT OF FOUR PARTS

Each section of this kit provides an overview of one of our five core principles, plus specific ways to get started:

ASK THIS
Diagnostic questions to answer before starting.

DO THIS
Must-do actions, organized around the three "key practices" that support each principle.

TRY THIS
Tips and tools to consider, suitable for some situations more than others.

READ THIS
The most helpful resources (mostly books) on topics related to each principle.

In this Starter Kit, we've worked hard to be selective rather than comprehensive. Since every strategic conversation is customized to context, we've honed in on the most general principles and practices that should apply to any situation. (Most points are covered in more detail in the corresponding chapters of the book.)

We hope that this Starter Kit will prove an invaluable resource for you. As you try out these ideas, please shoot us feedback on what's worked well and what you've learned along the way—so that we can learn from you, too!

BEFORE YOU BEGIN

ASK THIS

WHAT KIND OF STRATEGIC CONVERSATION DO YOU NEED?

DO YOU HAVE A MESSY, OPEN-ENDED, ILL-DEFINED STRATEGIC CHALLENGE WITH POTENTIALLY BIG CONSEQUENCES?

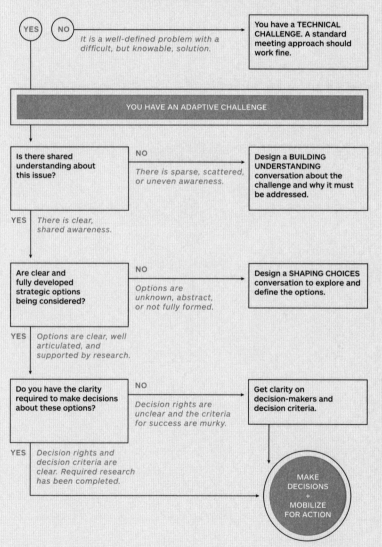

YES   NO   *It is a well-defined problem with a difficult, but knowable, solution.*

You have a TECHNICAL CHALLENGE. A standard meeting approach should work fine.

YOU HAVE AN ADAPTIVE CHALLENGE

Is there shared understanding about this issue?

NO   *There is sparse, scattered, or uneven awareness.*

Design a BUILDING UNDERSTANDING conversation about the challenge and why it must be addressed.

YES   *There is clear, shared awareness.*

Are clear and fully developed strategic options being considered?

NO   *Options are unknown, abstract, or not fully formed.*

Design a SHAPING CHOICES conversation to explore and define the options.

YES   *Options are clear, well articulated, and supported by research.*

Do you have the clarity required to make decisions about these options?

NO   *Decision rights are unclear and the criteria for success are murky.*

Get clarity on decision-makers and decision criteria.

YES   *Decision rights and decision criteria are clear. Required research has been completed.*

MAKE DECISIONS + MOBILIZE FOR ACTION

1

DEFINE
YOUR
PURPOSE

Most strategic conversations run for a day or two. But adaptive challenges can rarely be "solved" this quickly—even with intense effort. They're too complex.

Resolving an adaptive challenge requires a sustained effort over time—usually a few months or longer. This process comprises many activities, including informal discussions, research, planning sessions, formal review meetings, market experiments—and strategic conversations.

Strategic conversations often have an outsize impact on the success or failure of this larger process. The goal of any one session is to generate insights and energy that will create forward momentum. That's what makes for a true moment of impact—rather than an "okay" meeting or fun one-off event. When designing a strategic conversation, you need to understand where and how it fits into this larger process.

You also need to define the purpose of your session clearly. While there are infinite reasons to bring a group together, strategic conversations have only three purposes: Building Understanding, Shaping Choices, or Making Decisions.

To be effective, your strategic conversation must focus on one—and only one—of these goals. Once you decide which kind of session you're organizing, the design process becomes much clearer—and your odds of success increase significantly.

Which kind of strategic conversation do you need?

If your group doesn't know much about—or has divergent opinions on—the strategic issues on the table, you need to run a Building Understanding session. If they have tons of knowledge but are spinning their wheels, it's time for a Shaping Choices session. Only when you've done both of these well can you think about organizing a Making Decisions session.

Who has the ultimate decision rights?

For most routine organizational issues, decision rights are clear. With adaptive challenges, they can be maddeningly vague. That's because adaptive challenges typically cut across different parts of an organization and have no one "owner." To the extent possible, try to clarify before a session who will be responsible for making what kinds of decisions afterward. Otherwise there's a risk that no decisions will get made.

Who has lead responsibility for driving progress?

After a session is over, responsibility for maintaining momentum on an adaptive challenge can also be murky—for many of the same reasons that decision rights are unclear. Try to sort this out well before you enter the room.

What lessons can you learn from prior moments of impact?

Has your group had any aha moments in the past—the kind that spark new insight and alignment? Find out as much as you can about these moments. Study them. They're sure to yield important lessons that you can put to use in your session.

DO THIS

SEIZE YOUR MOMENT

Approach every strategic conversation as an opportunity to improve—or even transform—your organization's response to an adaptive challenge.

Start with a real question.

Great strategic conversations start with a question that's clear, relevant to your organization's future success, and that people are committed to doing something about. While it's fine to organize a session around an interesting topic or general issue, that's an executive-education or professional-development session—not a strategic conversation.

Establish boundary conditions.

Strategic conversations tend to stir up a lot of muck, not all of it relevant to the challenge at hand. Since many people see these sessions as an opportunity to take their hobbyhorses and pet peeves out for a ride, it's important to be clear about what issues are *not* on the table before you enter the room.

Reimagine victory.

The definition of victory is different for a strategic conversation than for a standard meeting. The goal of most meetings is to make decisions on next steps. The goal of a strategic conversation is to create alignment and generate new insights that can propel your organization forward. If you accomplish this, next steps are actually the easy part.

Plan for success.

Visualize your best-case scenario before heading into a strategic conversation. Ask yourself, "If this session goes really well, what kinds of actions can I imagine people taking soon after?" Sketch out a few initial plans on how you'll follow up on these actions. Taking this question seriously will make success more likely to happen—and you'll be better prepared when it does.

PICK ONE PURPOSE

There are only three reasons to have a strategic conversation: Building Understanding, Shaping Choices, or Making Decisions. Make sure you pick one—and only one—for your session.

WHEN BUILDING UNDERSTANDING

Pose a clear challenge—don't "tee up" issues.

It's hard to make progress on a big, broad topic like "the future of book publishing." When approaching a Building Understanding session, its best to give participants a clear challenge that will focus their attention and energy—such as coming up with innovative offerings, business models, or new insights into how readers' needs are changing.

Define the landing point.

One of the most difficult parts of a Building Understanding session is having a clear vision of how it will end—and how that ending will drive further progress. Before you walk into the room, you need to be clear about what kind of output you want—even though you can't know for sure what the content of that output will be. In the future-of-publishing example, you might define the landing point as three to five insights about the emerging needs of readers that can be used to develop new strategic options.

WHEN SHAPING CHOICES

Work with fully realized options.

"We should buy company X" is an idea, not a fully realized option. Turning it into one at a Shaping Choices session requires telling a compelling story about how the other company's offerings and capabilities could combine with yours to create real advantage. The best way to craft fully realized options is to use a rigorous framework or process—such as the Business Model Generation Canvas (shown on page 47)—to ensure that your story is coherent and complete.

Develop a manageable number of options.

In Shaping Choices sessions, it's usually best to work toward three to five well-developed options. Most people can't hold more than five options in their heads at the same time—that's too much complexity to manage. And working with just two options can lead to a polarized debate.

Focus on assumptions, not positions.

Take a hard look at the assumptions behind each option. Try asking, "What would we have to believe for each option to be successful?" This simple tactic usually shifts the discussion from personalities and positions to a frank assessment of the conditions required for success.

Treat the status quo as an explicit option.

People will gravitate toward the status quo if no other choice is made—even if few of them like it. When Shaping Choices, it's important to include the status quo path as an explicit option, subject to the same tests as possible new directions. This simple tactic will often encourage people to find a better choice.

GO SLOW TO GO FAST

Resolving adaptive challenges takes time, which is always in short supply. To succeed, you'll have to inspire your group to stick with it.

Manage expectations early and often.

Participants often have unrealistic expectations of what can be done at a strategic conversation—such as wanting to get to agreement on a strategy in just one day. You need to share your definition of victory for the session before people walk into the room. And be prepared to remind them of it several times during the session.

Resist attempts to rush downstream.

It's virtually guaranteed that participants will urge you to push the process further along than what makes sense. At a Building Understanding session, someone will likely try to go deeper into Shaping Choices territory. At a Shaping Choices session, you'll get pressure to start Making Decisions. Don't do it! Not only will you choke off the potential for critical insights, but once you move too far downstream, you might not have the option to move backward later.

Celebrate your "ahas."

You rarely know when lightning will strike at a strategic conversation—so be prepared to call it out forcefully when it does. Generating a sense of progress is critical to building the confidence and patience required to "go slow to go fast." When the group arrives at a major insight, make sure everyone knows it.

Get out of the office.

As writer John le Carré once wrote, "A desk is a dangerous place from which to view the world." Most of us spend too much time inside our organizations and not enough time looking around us. When designing a Building Understanding session, ask yourself what field trips you might include in your program that would give participants direct experience with the issues you'll be working on. If that's not practical, think about how to open the windows and doors and bring the outside world into your session.

Scan the periphery.

In his classic work *The Innovator's Dilemma*, Clayton Christensen points out that important changes usually appear first at the fringes of markets and organizations. Look around for early signs of change in different markets and units. You might find new ideas in surprising places.

Test-drive your options through different future environments.

We make important strategic choices based on today's data, but the results of these choices play out in the future. It's always helpful to stress-test your options across different environments—whether it's through simulations, scenario-planning exercises, or just putting each option through several rounds of asking "What if?"

Simulate the "new normal" inside your organization.

It's one thing to see a new strategy or set of policies on paper, and quite another to experience them in real life. Try creating a visceral sense of what it would feel like to operate under each direction. In choosing between a few strategic directions, the board of a large nonprofit reviewed the résumés of a short list of mock candidates for CEO and debated which one would be the best fit in each case.

Ask these five questions.

In their book *Playing to Win: How Strategy Really Works*, Roger Martin and A.G. Lafley describe a process for shaping and evaluating strategic choices built around five cascading questions, which together compel participants to develop sound options while also discussing the assumptions behind them:

1. *What is our winning aspiration?*

2. *Where will we play (e.g., what customers will we serve)?*

3. *How will we win (e.g., how will we deliver a unique value proposition to the market)?*

4. *What capabilities must be in place?*

5. *What management systems are required?*

READ THIS

CHIP HEATH AND DAN HEATH, *Switch: How to Change Things When Change Is Hard* (Crown Business, 2010). The Heath brothers combine in-depth research with engaging stories to illuminate key principles for making change happen in any context.

RONALD HEIFETZ AND MARTIN LINSKY, *Leadership on the Line: Staying Alive Through the Dangers of Leading* (Harvard Business Review Press, 2002). An excellent guide to how effective leaders work through adaptive challenges, ripe with implications for strategic conversations.

JOHN KOTTER, *Leading Change* (Harvard Business Review Press, 1996). The classic step-by-step primer on how to manage an organizational change process.

A.G. LAFLEY AND ROGER L. MARTIN, *Playing to Win: How Strategy Really Works* (Harvard Business Review Press, 2013). An indispensible guide for how to think about shaping and evaluating strategic options.

HENRY MINTZBERG, "The Fall and Rise of Strategic Planning," *Harvard Business Review*, January–February 1994, 107–14. This classic piece makes the case for the emergent approach to developing strategy—and explains why strategic planning doesn't work for really big issues.

JOHN MULLINS AND RANDY KOMISAR, *Getting to Plan B: Breaking Through to a Better Business Model* (Harvard Business Review Press, 2009). Venture capitalists know that entrepreneurs' Plan A strategies almost never work. This book is about how to pivot and find your Plan B.

ALEXANDER OSTERWALDER AND YVES PIGNEUR, *Business Model Generation: A Handbook for Visionaries, Game Changers, and Challengers* (Wiley, 2010). Nothing beats the BMG Canvas for working through new business model options.

BARRY SCHWARTZ, *The Paradox of Choice: Why More Is Less* (Ecco, 2003). People usually say they want more choices, but their behavior reveals that they want fewer. This work is loaded with lessons from social science research on how to think about shaping choices.

ROBERT SIMONS, *Seven Strategy Questions: A Simple Approach for Better Execution* (Harvard Business Review Press, 2010). A Harvard Business School professor lays out seven questions that need to be addressed in any strategy process.

2

ENGAGE
MULTIPLE
PERSPECTIVES

Adaptive challenges can't be solved without creative collaboration. You've got to get the right people—and perspectives—in the room working on the right problem in the right ways.

But there's a catch: strategic conversations can inhibit creative collaboration even as they demand it. That's because these sessions focus on uncertainties that can make participants uneasy, often trigger competitive impulses, and feature an element of personal performance that can spark anxiety.

There's a huge difference between a group that's going through the motions versus one that's really humming. Three key practices make most of the difference.

First, you've got to get a dream team of perspectives (not just people) in the room—one that's diverse in ways that matter to the challenge. Second, you must create a common platform for creative collaboration, without falling victim to groupthink. And third, you must find ways to turn up or down the heat to get the best out of participants.

Doing these things well will create a strong foundation for the rest of the process. But only if you do one more thing. Setting the right environment for creative collaboration requires deeply listening to participants well before the session starts. This will help you design choices that resonate with your group.

Which perspectives do you need to engage to solve your problem?

The best strategic conversations feature a well-chosen mix of perspectives and voices that will come at your challenge from a variety of angles. Keep in mind that not all of these voices need to be physically present.

What kind of group are you bringing together?

Once you've chosen your participants, study the roster. Is this a team with existing relationships or an ad hoc group assembled just for this session—or somewhere in between? The answer should influence many of your design choices.

What kinds of stress will this session create?

All strategic conversations are stressful for at least some participants. Think through the different kinds of stress that your session is likely to introduce, so that you can find ways to reduce them. Pay close attention to participants who are likely to feel most under pressure.

Which differences do you need to lean into?

Your participants' many differences—of role, of mind-set, of culture, and more—can be rich sources of insight. But these differences have to interact with one another in the right ways to create value. Given your challenge and your mix of participants, which differences can you accentuate to throw off valuable sparks?

DO THIS

ASSEMBLE A DREAM TEAM

The best strategic conversations get the dream team in the room, not the "must-invite team" of usual suspects. To get a dream team, you'll need to be more selective and more inclusive than usual.

Get the right perspectives—not just the right people.

It's important to separate the question of which *people* will be present in the room from which *perspectives* need to be represented. It's often helpful to get perspectives from people who can't be there in person— such as customers or subject-matter experts. Find creative ways—using video, audio, interviews, and so on—to get these fresh voices heard.

Find some "friends of ambiguity."

All strategic conversations require wrestling with uncertainty and ambiguity—conditions that some people are more comfortable with than others. It's important to have a critical mass of participants who operate well under these conditions. Otherwise, you're in for a bumpy ride.

Include a few hubs and connectors.

Make an effort to include participants who are well networked within your organization. They can play a valuable role at your session by building bridges between different subgroups in the room. Afterward, they can share insights with others who weren't there.

Engage perspectives from the frontier.

Important change almost always appears first at the edges of markets and organizations—from more remote geographies, newer consumers, younger workers, and the like. It's a good idea to include some of these frontier perspectives in your session.

Include the doers and the affected.

Great strategic ideas only matter if they are broadly accepted and well executed. When practical, it's good to include the perspectives of people who will be responsible for executing the options or who will be most affected by them.

CREATE A COMMON PLATFORM

Groups work best when they start with a critical mass of shared perspective.

Think of your platform as having eight key planks:

▸ A sense of shared purpose and objectives.

▸ A sense of group identity and community.

▸ A common understanding of the challenges.

▸ A sense of urgency.

▸ A shared language system or common definition of key terms.

▸ A shared base of information to draw upon.

▸ The capacity to discuss tough issues.

▸ Common frames through which to see the issues.

Figure out which part(s) of the platform need reinforcement.

You'll want to reinforce most or all of these planks. Does your group have a decent understanding of the challenges but lack a sense of urgency? Do they have a strong group identity but avoid tough topics? Depending on the purpose of your session and the nature of the group, you might need to secure a few of these planks with a strong hammer.

Use interview feedback for "level setting."

One of the most effective ways to get a session started is to share with participants their key areas of agreement and divergence, as discovered through pre-meeting interviews. This can save a huge amount of time by helping the group appreciate how much they're already aligned and allowing them to focus their energy on the areas that matter most.

IGNITE A CONTROLLED BURN

Once your group has a strong platform, it's time to lean into the areas where they're not aligned—and need to be.

Figure out if you need to crank up the heat or contain it.

Many groups either get stuck in debate mode—talking without listening—or avoid tough issues altogether. Think about whether your group needs more help raising the temperature and urgency around the core issues—or finding safe ways to channel the heat that they're already bringing to a session.

Choose your tactics for igniting a controlled burn.

Eight tactics work particularly well, individually or in combination:

▸ Take a longer time perspective on the issues.

▸ Take an "outside-in" perspective, focusing on external drivers of change.

▸ Turn the challenge into a game or simulation.

▸ Focus the discussion on key assumptions, not conclusions.

▸ Have people walk in the shoes of others.

▸ Make the group grapple with tough trade-offs.

▸ Agree on neutral criteria for making choices.

▸ Set and maintain clear boundaries and ground rules.

Give borderline attendees an interview option.

In most strategic conversations, there is serious pressure to include individuals whose contribution may be marginal. If you must invite them, consider giving them the option of providing their input through a pre-meeting interview. You might be surprised. While most people want to have a voice, not everyone wants to sacrifice a day or two for the cause.

Create a "cheat sheet" of key terms.

Having a common language system is critical to discussing challenges effectively. But there can be confusion about the meaning of even basic terms—such as vision, strategy, goals, and objectives—and how they relate to one another. It's often helpful to provide a glossary of key terms so that everyone can work from the same definitions. (It's less important that these definitions be "right"—which is often subjective—and more important that they be used consistently.)

Play the "gives and gets game."

The economic development agency Scottish Enterprise used this activity to kick off an important strategic conversation. Teams from different parts of the organization were asked to list all of their contributions to the other parts ("gives") as well as the benefits they received ("gets"). Results showed clearly that *all parts* believed they were contributing far more than they were receiving back from the others—a logical impossibility. Could your group use this game—or a similar one—to remind them that they're all in it together?

Get people to switch hats.

Sometimes the only way to see another person's viewpoint is to walk in his or her shoes. To create a better sense of roles and responsibilities among his new executive team, the leader of a large health-care organization had each member role-play the position of another team member during a decision-making exercise. The head of HR played the CFO, the chief counsel played a business unit leader, and so on. This tactic helped widen each person's perspective on the company's goals and strategies.

Find the hidden needs.

When working through an adaptive challenge, your group risks getting overwhelmed. That's where "needs finding," which designers employ to identify new ways to delight users, can come in handy. Needs finding can be as simple as asking all participants in advance how an upcoming session might be helpful to them. This can keep them focused on positive outcomes—and might uncover insights they would otherwise miss.

MAP the motivations.

In his book *Reading the Room*, psychologist David Kantor lays out a simple frame for seeing the range of motivations within a group. While each individual has a unique combination of motives, people tend to lead with one of three core values: meaning (or purpose), affect (or relationships), or power (hence MAP). A quick assessment of the MAP landscape in any group can inform your design, including what kinds of activities and language to use.

READ THIS

JUANITA BROWN, *World Café: Shaping Our Futures Through Conversations That Matter* (Berrett-Koehler Publishers, 2005). A seminal work on group-process design from a leader in organizational-development practice and theory.

EDWARD DE BONO, *Six Thinking Hats* (Back Bay Books, 1999). A succinct primer on the strengths of different ways of thinking—and how to bring them together for creative problem-solving.

BOB FRISCH, *Who's in the Room? How Great Leaders Structure and Manage the Teams Around Them* (Jossey-Bass, 2012). Reveals how decisions in organizations really get made (hint: it's not at executive committee meetings).

ART KLEINER, *Who Really Matters? The Core Group Theory of Power, Privilege, and Success* (Currency/Doubleday, 2003). A thorough and illuminating analysis of how organizational politics really works. You'll never again look at power dynamics the same.

JOHN KOTTER, *Buy-In: Saving Your Good Idea from Getting Shot Down* (Harvard Business Review Press, 2010). A compelling, story-based demonstration of how skillful navigation of different opinions can lead to group alignment.

PATRICK LENCIONI, *Death by Meeting: A Leadership Fable . . . About Solving the Most Painful Problem in Business* (Jossey-Bass, 2004). A reality-based novel about why so many meetings are so dreadful—and how mining conflict and having the right structure can fix them.

KERRY PATTERSON, JOSEPH GRENNY, RON MCMILLAN, AND AL SWITZLER, *Crucial Conversations: Tools for Talking When the Stakes Are High* (McGraw-Hill, 2011). An indispensable guide for thinking about how to manage difficult but necessary conversations.

DAVID ROCK, *The Brain at Work: Strategies for Overcoming Distraction, Regaining Focus, and Working Smarter All Day Long* (HarperBusiness, 2009). A fascinating review of recent findings in neuroscience as applied to our day jobs, with a host of implications for group collaboration.

DANIEL YANKELOVICH, *The Magic of Dialogue: Transforming Conflict into Cooperation* (Simon & Schuster, 1999). A helpful overview of the theory and practice of dialogue, from the renowned social scientist and pollster.

3

FRAME
THE
ISSUES

An important part of your job is to frame (and reframe) issues in ways that help your group "see" the same things at the same time.

As the word suggests, a *frame* is a strong focusing device. It determines which elements are inside versus outside your field of vision, and which are in the foreground versus the background. A well-defined frame strikes a fine balance: it focuses your attention while also lighting up your peripheral vision.

A frame can take many forms. It could be a visual image or map—such as a competitive landscape or investment portfolio matrix. It could be a metaphor or concept—such as "innovator's dilemma" or "tipping point"—that helps participants interpret a situation. It could be a "sticky" story that helps people make sense of different observations. Or it can even be the way you phrase the key question that you ask people to work on.

A few well-chosen frames can illuminate different aspects of the adaptive challenge you're wrestling with, including how the various parts relate to the whole. They help participants get their heads around a great deal of complexity, thereby accelerating insight and alignment. Having a strategic conversation without a strong frame (or two) is like trying to do a jigsaw puzzle without the picture on the box. It's possible—but damn hard.

What important frames are already in play?

Participants already have their own frames in place that shape their thinking about the issues you'll be discussing. Try to identify these existing frames—whether visual frames, metaphors, key concepts, buzzwords, or stories—in advance. Can these frames be useful? Or are they out-of-date? If so, do they need to be surfaced and challenged—and perhaps replaced?

What kinds of frames work well with this group?

Frames come in many flavors, and people have different tastes. Is your group visual, or are they more drawn to sticky stories? Are they more comfortable with two-by-two matrices or a catchy metaphor? Think about the memes that have captured your group's imagination in the past. What lessons can you draw from these memes that will help you choose frames for your session?

Do you need widening or narrowing frames?

Like a photographer's lenses, frames can either widen your perspective or narrow your focus. If the group is thinking too narrowly about their options or are stuck in groupthink, then you'll need widening frames. If they're overwhelmed by too much information or too many options, you'll want to develop frames that focus attention on what matters most.

Is an "invisible gorilla" in the room?

Most groups have blind spots—like the chest-thumping gorilla that many people don't see smack in the middle of Daniel Simons's famous video clip. What big issue is your group blind to—or ignoring on purpose? What kind of frame could make the gorilla in the room impossible to miss?

DO THIS

**KEY
PRACTICE
1**

STRETCH (DON'T BREAK) MIND-SETS

The best frames expand on participants' current perspectives, rather than opposing or replacing them outright.

Get into participants' heads.

Keep one eye on your content and one on your participants' mental models and assumptions. You'll need to work hard to understand their mental models through interviews or surveys even if you already know the group well.

Test your key frames in advance.

Few things can bring your strategic conversation to a halt faster than the rejection of one of your frames by a key participant—or the entire group. Always test your most important frames with a few well-chosen participants beforehand. Be sure not to cave too quickly when you encounter resistance; any new frame is likely to make some people uncomfortable at first. Use these tests to adjust your frames until they create the right amount of stretch between the familiar and the new.

Be open to alternative frames.

Allow time for participants to refine your frames or come up with their own. Even if you end up sticking with the originals, looking at the issues through a few different lenses could shake out some new insights. If the group can't find better frames, they'll buy in more strongly to the ones you've developed.

THINK INSIDE *DIFFERENT* BOXES

Telling people to "think outside the box" isn't specific enough to be helpful. Instead, give your group different boxes within which to think about their challenge.

What would a new entrant do?

When coming up with new ideas, it's almost always helpful to ask participants, "What would a new entrant to our industry do today if they didn't have our legacy systems and relationships?" Or you could try redesigning your company logo to resemble iconic brands—such as Google or Starbucks—and let these new logos inspire new, creative thinking among participants about how to reshape or play in their markets.

What if you had unlimited resources?

Participants often constrain their options without realizing it. They limit their ideas to things they can do without overturning any existing efforts or strategies. Inviting them to brainstorm options without such constraints can generate new ideas that might be more possible than first imagined.

What if you had severely limited resources?

Imposing new constraints can also unleash insights. You might ask, "How would we solve this problem if our budget were one-tenth what it is now?" This question challenges participants to think up scrappy, low-cost solutions, as many start-ups often have to do.

CHOOSE A FEW KEY FRAMES

A few select frames will help you organize your content, craft your agenda, and structure discussion in the room.

Limit your frames.

Having two or three key frames works best. Using too many in one session (Frameworkpalooza) can lead to more headaches than ideas. With a small number of frames, odds are higher that one will become "sticky" and help carry the group's momentum forward.

Identify your frames early.

It's critical to identify your frames well in advance because you'll want to organize your strategic conversation's content, agenda, and experience around them. Locking in your frames too late might mean last-minute changes to these elements. At the same time, you'll want to allow enough time to test your frames, so it's important not to set them in stone too early.

Show how your frames relate to one another.

If you use more than one key frame, it's guaranteed that someone will ask how the frames relate to one another. Ask this question of yourself beforehand—and make sure you have a good answer!

Identify—and break—industry orthodoxies.

Every industry has its own set of beliefs about how the world works—beliefs that are often challenged by entrepreneurs. Larry Keeley of the innovation-strategy consultancy Doblin likes to point out that the common practice of grocery stores offering express lanes for customers with small loads results in lower-priority service for their best customers. What orthodoxies does your industry or organization have that are worth challenging?

Widen the lens on competition.

Too often, groups take a narrow view on competition that focuses only on major players. Recent history is full of cases in which start-ups and entrants from other industries have wreaked havoc on orderly competitive markets. (Think of Amazon in book publishing.) What companies in adjacent spaces might be tempted to get into your markets—and how might that change the game?

Take a look at neglected customers.

In most industries, the big competitors tend to focus on the same high-profit customers. Yet some of the most successful innovations in recent years have targeted "less attractive" customers—or even noncustomers. In an already crowded field, Enterprise Rent-A-Car found a market providing insurance-claim rentals while Zipcar led the way in casual short-term rentals. Are there neglected corners of your markets that could become areas of growth?

Create vivid metaphors to capture the essence of the challenge.

Recall the Drip and the Avalanche. These few words became a valuable shorthand that helped leaders of a large Internet-service provider understand the market dynamics shaping the future of video-on-demand services. Experiment with a few images and metaphors that might succinctly capture larger dynamics of your challenge—and thus engage your group in its solution.

Mine the memes.

Write down all the buzzwords and memes that have currency in your organization today. Then review the list and ask whether one or more of these might be deployed in your session.

Try sketching out the problem—and its solution.

In *The Back of the Napkin*, Dan Roam asserts that complex problems can be not just depicted but solved through simple pictures. If you know which of six core questions you're really asking—who and what, how much, where, when, how, or why—then you know what sort of sketch or picture to draw. Use Roam's approach to explore what visual frames you might use at your session.

Play around with the Duarte Diagrammer.

Duarte Design's online Diagrammer tool offers a few thousand examples of how to visualize an issue (www.duarte.com). It's a helpful resource for getting visual inspiration that could make your frames come alive.

READ THIS

DANIEL ARIELY, *Predictably Irrational: The Hidden Forces That Shape Our Decisions* (Harper-Perennial, 2010). A fascinating and at times hilarious exposé of hardwired human folly that shows how our internal frames can get in our way.

STEPHEN DENNING, *The Springboard: How Storytelling Ignites Action in Knowledge-Based Organizations* (Butterworth-Heinemann, 2001). Defines a specific genre of stories that people can use as "springboards" for their own goals.

NANCY DUARTE, *Resonate: Present Visual Stories That Transform Audiences* (Wiley, 2010). A breakthrough work that reveals the underlying structure of the stories that burrow into our imagination.

CHIP HEATH AND DAN HEATH, *Made to Stick: Why Some Ideas Survive and Others Die* (Random House, 2007). A handy formula for crafting catchy stories that people will remember.

CHIP HEATH AND DAN HEATH, *Decisive: How to Make Better Choices in Life and Work* (Crown Business, 2013). Features clear, research-based guidance on framing issues and choices in ways that lead to better decisions.

DANIEL KAHNEMAN, *Thinking, Fast and Slow* (Farrar, Straus and Giroux, 2011). A power tour of three decades of research on behavioral economics and cognitive biases, from the Nobel Prize–winning social psychologist.

MICHAEL MAUBOUSSIN, *Think Twice: Harnessing the Power of Counterintuition* (Harvard Business Press Review, 2009). A leading wealth manager shares the habits—and power—of contrarian thinking, with ample lessons for the pragmatic strategist.

BARRY NALEBUFF AND IAN AYRES, *Why Not? How to Use Everyday Ingenuity to Solve Problems Big and Small* (Harvard Business School Press, 2003). Filled with nifty, real-world examples of the power of creative framing and reframing.

DAN ROAM, *The Back of the Napkin: Solving Problems and Selling Ideas with Pictures* (Portfolio, 2008). A hands-on course in visual framing and problem-solving. No drawing skills required beyond stick figures.

TIHAMÉR VON GHYCZY, "The Fruitful Flaws of Strategy Metaphors," *Harvard Business Review*, September 2003, 86–94. An elegant explanation of how metaphors inform strategic conversations—and how they differ from models.

2 ENGAGE MULTIPLE PERSPECTIVES

3 FRAME THE ISSUES

DEFINE YOUR PURPOSE

1

5 MAKE IT AN EXPERIENCE

4 SET THE SCENE

4

SET THE SCENE

Walk into the room in which a strategic conversation will take place, and you'll quickly pick up subtle cues about what's about to happen—for better or worse.

Is the room set up for open dialogue or passive listening? Are the tables and chairs arranged to reinforce hierarchy or to level it? Do the small touches signal that this is a special event where anything could happen—or just another day at work? Is this a room where people will do hard work together—or just multitask side by side?

Most people can suss out the above in mere seconds, just by seeing how the scene has been set. Unfortunately, what they see is usually not encouraging or inspiring.

Meeting organizers ask themselves over and over, Do we have everything we need? Strategic conversation designers ask a different question first: Where and how can we create the best environment for creative collaboration? They're fussy about picking the right kind of space—and then work hard to make it their own. They create opportunities to tap into visual thinking throughout the session. And they obsess over nailing the details.

It's possible to set a great scene at any budget level and in any space that's got the basics right (see page 217 for our checklist of basic requirements). Doing so requires taking personal responsibility for the total environment in which participants will be working. Strategic conversation designers don't just do this because it's nice: they know from experience that it can make a huge difference to the final outcome.

What first impression do you want to make?

The moment participants walk into a strategic conversation, they start calibrating their expectations based on what they see. What specific thoughts and feelings do you want them to have at that moment? Do you want them to feel curious or reassured? Ready to think in a focused way or more expansively? The scene they walk into should create expectations that align with your session's purpose.

Which constraints can you turn into advantages?

You'll have to deal with constraints of some kind in designing your session. When they arise, think like a designer and turn them to your advantage. When Gervais Tompkin of Gensler had only a half day to get through numerous big decisions with a group, he and his team banned all shades of gray (i.e., nuance) from the discussion. To underscore the point, the team dubbed their session "The Black and White Meeting" and set a two-tone scene with the materials and even the clothes they wore.

Which kinds of visuals will best help your group see a solution?

It's easier for people to come together around the same ahas when they literally see the same thing at the same time. Many kinds of visual interfaces—from flip charts and digital Smart Boards to sketches and prototypes—can get you there. You might use several in your session, but usually just one or two visuals will stick with participants. Be thoughtful about which interfaces you choose to deploy—and why.

What small touches could make a big impact?

Great designers know that small details often define the user experience—such as the way instruments are laid out for a surgeon or the subtle feedback sounds a smartphone makes when you plug in the charger. Take a hard look at the scene that you're setting and ask, What are some small features that could delight participants and get them more engaged?

DO THIS

MAKE YOUR SPACE

Most meeting places are dull and ill suited for creative collaboration. We can—and must—do better.

Get out of Dodge.

When choosing a venue, it's best to get away from distractions or reminders of daily pressures. Creative breakthroughs rarely occur in the same conference room where you do budget reviews or project planning. If you must gather in a familiar and uninspiring space, do whatever you can to transform it—and signal that this session is different and important.

Start with a good "shell space."

A few venue basics are important to get right. Before you start doing anything fancy, make sure you've got a good shell space that supports creative collaboration. At a minimum, this includes an appropriate-size room with movable furniture and ample space for generating and sharing ideas.

Fight for natural light!

Studies show that patients recover better from surgery if they're in rooms with windows. Natural light has a big impact on mood and energy levels in any setting—and it's a critical requirement for any session that's a half day or longer. When you're booking a space, some meeting planners will claim this doesn't matter and steer you toward the nearest cave. Don't do it!

Customize to context.

Once you have a shell space, think about how to make it your own in ways that are consistent with your purpose. It often helps to come up with a unifying theme or two to guide your design choices. When Amway designed a strategic conversation on the future of their global network of distributors, they set their scene around three themes, each with its own space: a café, a viewing area, and a crafts studio. As participants rotated through them, the distinct spaces put people in the right frame of mind for dialogue, taking in information, and generating ideas, respectively.

Room 101

Pick a room that works . . .

- *Size:* Doesn't feel cramped or cavernous.
- *Shape:* Allows everyone to see and be easily seen.
- *Space:* Works well for both plenary and breakout sessions (which may or may not be in separate rooms), with ample open space.
- *Windows:* Let the sunshine in!

And can be easily adapted . . .

- *Furniture:* Movable, supporting quick set changes as needed.
- *Writing surface:* Gives participants space to write, doodle, and work out ideas on paper.
- *Clear wall space:* Enough to hang posters, timelines, templates, or other materials that need to be visible at all times.

And is comfortable and free from distractions . . .

- *Seating:* Comfy and breathable.
- *Room temperature:* Controllable and reasonably set.
- *Acoustics:* Everyone can hear everyone else clearly, with no distracting noises in the background.
- *Minimal visual distractions:* No visual craziness such as psychedelic carpets, bad art, cluttered storage piles, or busy traffic.

GET VISUAL

Our brains process images more readily than text. Tap into the power of visuals to help your group get to insights faster.

Support words with images (not more words).

Never ask people to listen to a presentation and read words on a screen at the same time. Research shows that our brains can't hack it. Instead, populate your slides or other visuals with images that reinforce what you're trying to communicate—and minimal text.

Use visual frameworks to see the forest *and* the trees.

Discussions about complex topics tend to either stay too abstract or get mired in details. To see the forest and the trees at the same time, create or find a simple visual framework that helps your group connect individual observations or ideas back to the bigger-picture challenge. Keep this frame visible throughout the session.

Capture and display key points in the conversation.

When key points are captured visually, they're more likely to be remembered and picked up again later. And when participants' ideas have been heard and recorded in this way, they are more likely to let go of past points and focus on the present conversation.

Build a concrete record of progress.

Capturing key points visually also helps give people a sense of momentum—they can literally see the insights and agreements building over time. You don't want to clutter the walls with every bit of data, but carefully curate which artifacts (e.g., flip chart drawings, completed templates, lists of agreements) will best support the conversation and build a sense of progress.

Visual Elements to a Strategic Conversation

In designing your session, think about where, when, and how you can use these visual tools to get to more concrete ideas:

- *Prepared materials:* All premade materials that put a visual stamp on a session, such as slides, posters, handouts, or timelines.

- *Process templates:* Worksheets or templates designed to help guide participants through a series of steps.

- *Frameworks:* Visual models that help structure conversation and connect individual issues to a larger challenge; these can be as simple as a timeline or as complex as a systems diagram.

- *Prototypes:* Drawings or other renderings of working-draft ideas and solutions; these can be low resolution or highly polished, created in advance or live.

- *Live capture:* Flip charts, graphic recordings, photographs, and digital interfaces (such as a wiki) that capture and curate content in real time.

- *Emergent sketches:* Any visual interface used for real-time exploration and idea building, such as mind mapping, doodling, or a graffiti wall.

DO SWEAT THE SMALL STUFF

In design, the delight is in the details. When all the small parts of a program come together, it gets people's attention.

Banish all possible distractions.

People are easy to distract. Most of the time, we'll take any excuse to avoid concentrating. This means having your core supplies, technology, and seating all set up in advance. It also means no piles of supplies or other visual clutter in the corner of the room; no noisy traffic or construction nearby; no rooms that feel like iceboxes or ovens; and no wafting odors of food before the next meal's due.

Coddle your guests.

People who feel comfortable and cared for are more apt to relax their guard and expand their field of vision. Ways to help people get to this happy place include great food, a cozy space with a good view, or a small, appropriate gift.

Make all touch points congruent.

The scene should be free of any details that contradict your purpose. If your session is about sustainability, don't serve water in plastic bottles. If it's about working better across organizational silos, ditch the big conference table (or anything else) that cuts people off from one another. If it's about moving forward boldly into the future, it's best not to gather in a place that reeks of the past.

Make sure all templates are the right size.

It's hard to capture big ideas on tiny pieces of paper. Visual templates or worksheets should be the right size for the number of people working on them. For one or two people, notebook-size paper or a bit larger works fine. For groups of three or more, you'll need anywhere from a eleven-by-seventeen-inch template to a four-by-eight-foot space.

Consider a nontraditional venue.

Most strategic conversations are held in office buildings or hotels. It's worth considering less obvious options. We've run strategic conversations in a nightclub, a cruise ship, a baseball-stadium skybox, an art gallery, and even a convent. While such venues may require more logistical lifting, they can also deliver an element of surprise and a more direct connection to your theme.

Create a "graffiti wall" timeline.

One powerful way to establish shared context is to create a large visual timeline of relevant trends and events. For a strategic conversation on impact investing, the Rockefeller Foundation posted a timeline showing how different forces had come together over the prior decade to bring the field into existence. They also invited participants to add their personal stories to it—like a graffiti wall—placing themselves within the bigger picture.

Pack a sound track.

Music may be the most overlooked tool for strategic scene-setting. A sound track can give your session a sense of forward motion and serve as an "aural curtain" to signal when intermissions begin and end. Just make sure your music choices aren't out of sync with the tone of the session or the group culture.

Bring the outside world in.

Organizations tend to be insular and inward looking. A colleague of ours brought the outside world into a strategic conversation on customer service by playing real recordings from the company's call center as background "white noise" during session breaks. Gensler's Gervais Tompkin did it by bringing into his session life-size cutout figures of important individuals who couldn't be there in person. These clever moves turn the old saying inside out: "in sight, in mind."

Use "graphic guides" to find your way.

Small groups tend to be more productive when they have an attractive visual template or process map to help organize the discussion. The Grove consulting group calls these "graphic guides" and features a wide variety of them on their website, which can either be used off the shelf or as inspiration to create your own (www.grove.com).

Brand it!

Sometimes it makes sense to create a distinct brand for a session. This needn't be complicated or expensive—a basic logo can do the trick. Creating a visual image of your theme and a consistent color palette can help tie together different elements of your program.

Take it easy with the toys.

Tossing a bunch of toys on the table—yo-yos, sculpting clay, and so on—can be a nice touch when asking people to get creative. But it also runs the risk of trivializing the proceedings. While creative problem-solving should involve a good dose of serious play, toys are not always the way to go. Try to think of less obvious ways to inject a bit of practical fun.

SCOTT DOORLEY AND SCOTT WITTHOFT, *Make Space: How to Set the Stage for Creative Collaboration* (Wiley, 2012). The two Scotts had the privilege—and challenge—of designing the facility for the Institute of Design at Stanford. This book shares their best practices for building creative workspaces.

NANCY DUARTE, *Slide:ology: The Art and Science of Creating Great Presentations* (O'Reilly Media, 2008). A valuable primer on how to create slides and other materials that engage rather than bore, with lessons for novices and masters alike.

STEVEN FEW, *Show Me the Numbers: Designing Tables and Graphs to Enlighten,* 2nd ed. (Analytics Press, 2012), and *Now You See It: Simple Visualization Techniques for Quantitative Analysis* (Analytics Press, 2009). An excellent introduction to data visualization, drawing on Edward Tufte's groundbreaking work and presented in an accessible style.

DON NORMAN, *The Design of Everyday Things* (Basic Books, 2002). In this classic work of design criticism, Norman plumbs the depths of why and how things—and environments—delight or drive us to despair.

GARR REYNOLDS, *Presentation Zen: Simple Ideas on Presentation Design and Delivery,* 2nd ed. (New Riders, 2011). The bestselling bible on delivering text-light, image-centric presentations.

DAN ROAM, *Blah, Blah, Blah: What to Do When Words Don't Work* (Portfolio Hardcover, 2011). Roam's first book, *The Back of the Napkin,* showed how simple sketches can help people get to creative solutions faster. This one goes into much more detail about how visual thinking can enable better conversations.

DAVID SIBBET, *Visual Meetings: How Graphics, Sticky Notes, and Idea Mapping Can Transform Group Productivity* (Wiley, 2010). Sibbet is known as the father of graphic facilitation—the practice of real-time visual capture of group discussions. His book lays out the key methods, with many useful tips for strategic conversations.

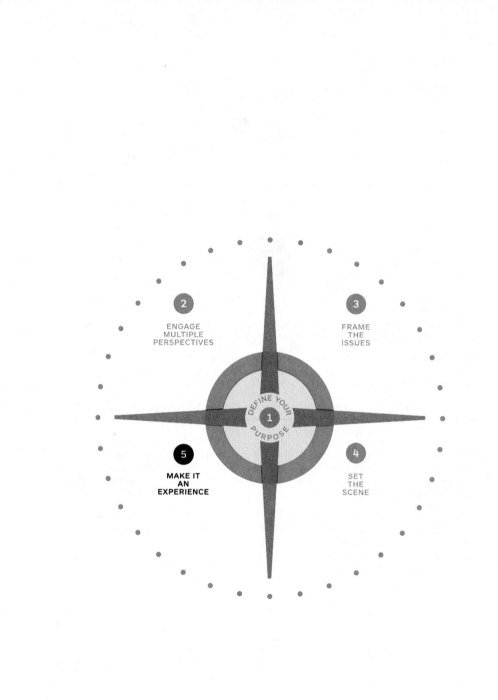

5

MAKE IT AN EXPERIENCE

Most people prep for a strategic conversation as if it were an important meeting—rather than a different kind of meeting altogether.

They approach the planning as an air-traffic controller might, trying to arrange landing slots for a slew of topics on an already packed agenda.

If you want to design a great experience—not just crank out an agenda—you'll need to adopt a different mind-set. Ditch the air-traffic controller headset and think instead like a deejay, choosing and sequencing your set list of activities in ways that will energize the crowd, tell a story, and make a mark.

Many people think of "experience" as a nice-to-have extra layer—like kicking off a session with a pleasant dinner, finding a great off-site venue, or making sure the meeting materials look pretty. But great experiences involve far more than one-off touches. They take people on an intellectual and emotional journey.

When designing your strategic conversation, you'll want to promote active learning; engage participants' hearts and guts (not just their minds); and create a strong narrative arc. Do these things well and you'll create an experience that leads to insight and action.

ASK THIS

What kind of experience does this group need now?

"Experience is the best teacher" may be a cliché—but it's true. Depending on your objectives, the right experience might be a war-gaming exercise, scenario-planning workshop, "deep dive" learning journey, customized simulation, or something else. Chances are it won't be a standard meeting packed with slide presentations.

How much should you focus on gain versus pain?

All strategic conversations pose a mix of gain (opportunities) and pain (risks), and groups can be more motivated by one or another. A well-designed session strikes a good psychological balance between the two that's suited to the specific situation and objectives.

How will your session make people comfortable—and uncomfortable?

Strategic conversations involve a balancing act that we call the *comfort paradox*. People are most creative when their basic needs are met and they aren't under stress. But arriving at new ideas always requires a bit of friction. Think through in advance the ways your session might make people feel both comfortable and uncomfortable.

What story do you want people to carry forward?

Every strategic conversation has a narrative arc. Think about the story (not just the "output") that you want people to leave with and then work backward from there in your design work. If that story includes visual images, it'll be easier for participants to remember and share with others.

DISCOVER, DON'T TELL

People learn best when they discover for themselves—yet another reason why we should stop shooting bullet points at one another.

Minimize time spent in live-content "downloads."

Make space for active learning. Take a hard look at all the content you plan to include to see how much of it you can distribute in advance as pre-readings or video "pre-watches" or turn into discovery-oriented activities. Your program can still include presentations, but keep them to a minimum so that participants don't get passive.

Maximize time spent in concrete problem-solving activities.

People get motivated when they're solving problems they care about—so be sure to weave several problem-solving activities into your session. Give breakout groups clear guidance, predesigned visual templates, or both to help them think and work together in structured ways.

Get people moving—and using their hands.

When Intuit's Kaaren Hanson wanted to help her colleagues understand how important it was for customers to have a positive "first use" of their products, she didn't lecture them about it. Instead, she handed them a few different types of combination locks to try using right out of the package, some of which were easy and others frustrating. This way, they could experience for themselves the impact that first use has on their own customers.

ENGAGE THE WHOLE PERSON

Reason and emotion aren't at odds—they're deeply interconnected. Great strategic conversations engage hearts and minds equally.

Create the conditions for human interaction.

Cold, formal environments invite stiff interactions. But you can't have genuine conversations without real emotion. If you want participants to engage as whole people, feature warm touches in the experience that signal to participants that it's okay to be fully human. This can be as simple as having cozy furniture, hand-drawn illustrations, or warm food. One group we worked with always served soup for lunch at their sessions because it made everyone feel better.

Set some clear boundaries.

Session hosts are often reluctant to invite emotion into the room because this can make a strategic conversation less predictable. Not all guests are comfortable with it, either. As you create the conditions for genuine dialogue, you also need to make design choices that set some boundaries to reassure these skeptics. One effective tactic is to establish neutral criteria for making choices at the session, which signals to participants that decisions will not end up being made by passion alone.

Prepare for the emotional highs—and lows.

The best conversations almost always feature both. As you saw in the story about the Christian Brothers in Australia coming to grips with their declining numbers, sometimes you need to orchestrate an emotional nosedive to make real progress. Groups that go through a catharsis together can often get to some amazing places on the other side.

CREATE A NARRATIVE ARC

An agenda is just a list, but an experience has flow and trajectory. Think through in advance how participants will experience your session as it unfolds.

Focus on beginnings and ends.

First impressions and closure are critical elements of any experience. Thanks to *peak-end bias*—a well-proven phenomenon in social psychology—we tend to remember best what happens last. Spend a disproportionate amount of your prep time coming up with great ways to open and close your session.

Work hard on the "crunch points."

The discipline of design asks you to focus on the "hardest things to get right" in any experience. In strategic conversations, some of the hardest things to get right are the moments when your group has to make a decision. Spend extra time and energy planning how to manage these moments of convergence.

Alternate activities for action and reflection.

Strategic conversations pulse back and forth between action and reflection. Think about how much hands-on work your group can do before they need to take a step back—and how much chitchat they'll tolerate before getting back to hands-on work. The best pacing is different for every group, but getting it right will keep your story moving forward.

Balance structure and antistructure.

Many strategic conversations flounder because they wander aimlessly around the issues or because they're a forced march through a thick jungle of content. Find a good balance between structure and antistructure. This means setting clear objectives, boundaries, and processes for making systematic progress—while also leaving enough flexibility for exploration and discovery.

Use the Doblin Five-E Model.

The design team at the innovation consultancy Doblin uses this simple tool for thinking systematically about any user experience.

THE DOBLIN FIVE-E MODEL FOR COMPELLING EXPERIENCES

1 ENTICE **How participants learn about the session in advance**

2 ENTER **How they arrive at the venue and room**

3 ENGAGE **How they experience the session**

4 EXIT **How they leave the venue and room**

5 EXTEND **All related communications and interactions (formal and informal) that follow the session**

Most people spend the most time thinking about 3—the event itself. But the other four stages are also critical to the participant experience. Small touches such as a creative invitation to the event (Entice) or an unusual gift (Exit and Extend) can make a big difference in participants' experience—and lasting memory—of a session.

Draw a "journey map."

Every strategic conversation has ebbs and flows of energy and emotion. Some of these are built into the program. Others grow spontaneously out of group dynamics. The diagram on page 136 in the chapter "Make It an Experience" offers an example of a simple "journey map" of the energy flows during one strategic conversation. Try sketching a simple graph like this showing how you think the session will feel from the participants' perspective.

Turn your challenge into a game.

A fun, learning-oriented game can be the easiest way to get people engaged. The Christian Brothers tackled their challenge of declining numbers with a Demography in Action board game, and Intuit's execs gained alignment around the need to fully embrace mobile devices through an engaging scavenger hunt. While such "gamification" may feel risky at first, you can reduce the risk by prototyping and testing the experience in advance.

Conduct a "prebrief" experience audit.

A common tool of the quality movement championed by W. Edwards Deming is the "prebrief"—or debrief of something that hasn't yet happened, to root out errors before they occur. Try running a prebrief of your session by asking "Imagine the session was a total flop—why was that?" and "Imagine that the session was a huge success—why was that?" You're sure to find a few ideas for how to improve your session.

Use a "headlines only" template for report-outs.

Small-group report-outs—where subsets of participants share their ideas or ahas with the larger group—can be the trickiest parts of a workshop. Participants often have trouble summarizing the work or conversation from their group and tend to meander. Give them a tight template—with room for headlines only—for reporting out their results.

READ THIS

JOHN D. BRADFORD, ANN L. BROWN, AND RODNEY R. COCKING, eds., *How People Learn: Brain, Mind, Experience, and School* (National Academies Press, 2000). This landmark National Research Committee report is a great starting point for learning about learning.

LEWIS P. CARBONE, *Clued In: How to Keep Customers Coming Back Again and Again* (FT Press, 2004). A comprehensive overview of how to think about experience design for products and services, with implications for strategic conversations.

DAVE GRAY, SUNNI BROWN, AND JAMES MACANUFO, *Gamestorming: A Playbook for Innovators, Rulebreakers, and Changemakers* (O'Reilly Media, 2010). A tool kit full of productive game-based activities to help groups generate new ideas. You can use the activities off the shelf or as a springboard for designing your own.

JOHN MEDINA, *Brain Rules: 12 Principles for Surviving and Thriving at Work, Home, and School* (Pear Press, 2008). Medina's overview of recent brain science is packed with relevant insights for thinking about how strategic conversations are experienced.

DONALD A. NORMAN, *Emotional Design: Why We Love (or Hate) Everyday Things* (Basic Books, 2005). A prominent design critic and psychologist shows how designers think about their craft from a holistic and human-centric perspective. Form and function, unite!

B. JOSEPH PINE II AND JAMES H. GILMORE, *The Experience Economy*, updated ed. (Harvard Business Review Press, 2011). The authors make a case for the importance of experience in today's economy and take readers on a tour of companies that get it right.

DANIEL PINK, *A Whole New Mind: Why Right-Brainers Will Rule the Future* (Riverhead Books, 2005). Part polemic and part how-to manual, Pink's bestseller explores the creative skills—such as storytelling, empathy, and design—that are reshaping our economy as well as our strategic conversations.

DANIEL SCHACTER, *Seven Sins of Memory: How the Mind Forgets and Remembers* (Mariner Books, 2002). This fascinating primer on the key features—and bugs—of human memory explains why and what we remember (or don't) after a moment has passed.

NOTES

INTRODUCTION: THE MOST IMPORTANT LEADERSHIP SKILL THEY
DON'T TEACH AT HARVARD BUSINESS SCHOOL (OR ANYWHERE ELSE)

1. Interview with Neil Grimmer, January 25, 2012.
2. Campbell's Soup Company press release, June 13, 2013, http://investor.camp bellsoupcompany.com/phoenix.zhtml?c=88650&p=irol-newsArticle_Print&ID =1829771&highlight=.
3. Patrick Lencioni, *Death by Meeting: A Leadership Fable . . . About Solving the Most Painful Problem in Business* (Jossey-Bass, 2004).
4. Keith Sawyer, *Collaborative Genius: The Creative Power of Collaboration* (Basic Books, 2007), 60.
5. The term VUCA originated in the US military in the late 1990s.
6. Ashlee Vance, "A Tiny Camcorder Has a Big Payday," *New York Times*, March 20, 2009; Sam Grobart and Evelyn M. Rusli, "For Flip Video Camera, Four Years from Hot Start-Up to Obsolete," *New York Times*, April 12, 2011; David Pogue, "The Tragic Death of the Flip," *New York Times* blog (Pogue's Posts), April 14, 2011.
7. Ronald Heifetz, *Leadership Without Easy Answers* (Belknap, 1994); Ronald Heifetz and Marty Linsky, *Leadership on the Line: Staying Alive through the Dangers of Leading* (Harvard Business Review Press, 2002); Ronald Hiefetz, Marty Linsky, and Alexander Grashow, *The Practice of Adaptive Leadership: Tools and Tactics for Changing Your Organization and the World* (Harvard Business Review Press, 2009).

8. Henry Mintzberg, *The Rise and Fall of Strategic Planning* (Free Press, 1994).

9. Richard Rumelt, *Good Strategy/Bad Strategy: The Difference and Why It Matters* (Crown Business, 2011), 4–5.

DESIGNING A STRATEGIC CONVERSATION

1. Natura company background from Wikipedia entry as of April 15, 2013.

2. Interview with Marcelo Cardoso, April 12, 2012.

3. Art Kleiner, "The Man Who Saw the Future," *strategy+business* 30 (Spring 2003); Art Kleiner, *The Age of Heretics: Heroes, Outlaws, and the Forerunners of Corporate Change* (Currency Doubleday, 1996): 139–80; Herman Kahn, *Thinking the Unthinkable in the 1980s* (Touchstone, 1985).

4. Interview with Napier Collyns, September 21, 2011.

5. Pierre Wack, "Scenarios: Shooting the Rapids," *Harvard Business Review*, November–December 1985, 140.

6. Pierre Wack, *Scenarios: The Gentle Art of Re-perceiving: One Thing or Two Learned While Developing Planning Scenarios for Royal Dutch/Shell*, vol. 9 of Working Paper (Harvard University, Graduate School of Business Administration, Division of Research, 1984).

7. Kleiner, "Man Who Saw"; Kleiner, *Age of Heretics*, 139–80.

8. Information about Wack's work at Shell and his legacy comes from cited publications plus interviews with former colleagues Napier Collyns (September 21, 2011, and May 18, 2012), Peter Schwartz (October 11, 2011, and February 21, 2013), and Kees van der Heijden (March 30, 2013).

9. Despite his stature, Wack left behind a surprisingly small body of published work—mainly two classic articles in *Harvard Business Review* in the fall of 1985. However, as best we can tell, he didn't coin the term *strategic conversation* as we use it here. This appears to have been crystallized as a term of art in conversations among the scenario planning team at Shell shortly after his tenure and was given wider currency by scenario practitioners at Global Business Network (cofounded by Shell alumni) in the mid-1990s. The term appears in publications in 1996 in two places: the subtitle of a book by Kees van der Heijden, *Scenarios: The Art of Strategic Conversation*, and the afterword of the paperback edition of Peter Schwartz's book *The Art of the Long View*. (An extended conversation between van der Heijden and Schwartz on this topic is in the preface to the second edition of *Scenarios: The Art of Strategic Conversation*, published by Wiley in 2005.) Still, while the term may not originate with him, Wack is clearly the intellectual godfather of many core concepts in the art of strategic conversation.

10. *New York Times*, "Taking Its Place Among the Largest Companies," February 25, 2012.

11. See http://www.gehealthcare.com/promo/advseries/index.html.

12. See Roger Martin, "Design Thinking Comes to the US Army," *Design Observer* blog, http://changeobserver.designobserver.com/feature/design-thinking-comes -to-the-us-army/13478/; and Colonel Stefan J. Banach, "Educating by Design: Preparing Leaders for a Complex World," *Military Review*, March–April 2009.

13. Jeanne Liedtka, "In Defense of Strategy as Design," *California Management Review*, 2000.

DEFINE YOUR PURPOSE

1. Based on Michael Lewis's *Moneyball: The Art of Winning an Unfair Game*, 1st ed. (W. W. Norton, April 2004). The movie *Moneyball* was released in 2011 by Columbia Pictures. *Moneyball* © 2011 Columbia Picture Industries, Inc. All Rights Reserved. Courtesy of Columbia Pictures.

2. See, for example, Mihaly Csikszentmalyi, *Creativity: Flow and the Psychology of Invention* (Harper Perennial, 1996), especially chapter 4: "The Work of Creativity," 77–106.

3. Interview with Ana Meade, February 24, 2012.

4. A.G. Lafley, Roger L. Martin, Jan W. Rivkin, and Nikolaj Sigglekow, "Bringing Science to the Art of Strategy," *Harvard Business Review*, September 2012, 4.

5. Bill Buxton, *Sketching User Experiences: Getting the Design Right and the Right Design* (Morgan Kaufmann, 2007).

6. Interviewees from Toyota Financial Services include George Borst, Ann Bybee, Julia Wada, Chris Ballinger, Ron Harris, Lisa Chen, Randall Borud, Mark Simmons, and Patrick van der Pijl (all on January 28, 2013).

7. See Roger Martin and A.G. Lafley, *Playing to Win: How Strategy Really Works*. The process described in this book was initially developed by Martin and colleagues at Monitor Group in the early 1990s.

8. For a more detailed explanation of why official leadership teams rarely make big strategic decisions in open, collaborative dialogue—in any kind of organization—see Bob Frisch's fine book *Who's in the Room? How Great Leaders Structure and Manage the Teams Around Them* (Jossey-Bass, 2012), or Art Kleiner's classic *Who Really Matters? The Core Group Theory of Power, Privilege, and Success* (Currency/Doubleday, 2003).

9. The concept of creative destruction in a modern, dynamic economy was articulated by Joseph A. Schumpeter in *Capitalism, Socialism, and Democracy*, first published in 1942.

10. The other four learning styles in Kolb's model are Diverging, Assimilating, Accommodating, and Balanced. See Sara L. Beckman and Michael Barry, "Teaching Students Problem Framing Skills with a Storytelling Metaphor," *International Journal of Engineering Education* 28, no. 2, 364–73.

11. Teresa Amabile and Steven Kramer, *The Progress Principle: Using Small Wins to Ignite Joy, Engagement, and Creativity at Work* (Harvard Business Review Press, 2011).

ENGAGE MULTIPLE PERSPECTIVES

1. Interview with Eamonn Kelly, July 12, 2012.

2. *Groupthink* was first coined by social psychologist Irving Janis as a condition that occurs when a group makes faulty decisions because group pressures lead to a deterioration of "mental efficiency, reality testing, and moral judgment." Irving Janis, *Victims of Groupthink* (New York: Houghton Mifflin, 1972).

3. Gregory Moorehead, Richard Ference, and Chris Neck, "Group Decision Fiascoes Continue: Space Shuttle *Challenger* and a Revised Groupthink Framework," *Human Relations* 44, no. 6 (1991): 539–50.

4. See, for example, Andrew Hargadon, *How Breakthroughs Happen: The Surprising Truth About How Companies Innovate* (Harvard Business School Press, 2003); Steven Johnson, *Where Good Ideas Come From: The Natural History of Innovation* (Riverhead Books, 2010); and Scott E. Page, *The Difference: How the Power of Diversity Creates Better Groups, Firms, Schools, and Societies* (Princeton University Press, 2007). On global innovation via YouTube, see Chris Anderson's TED talk "How Web Video Powers Global Innovation," filmed July 2010, posted September 2010, http://www.ted.com/talks/lang/en/chris_anderson_how_web_video _powers_global_innovation.html.

5. Steven Johnson, *Where Good Ideas Come From: The Natural History of Everything* (Riverhead Books, 2010), 33.

6. The classic study on how professionals find jobs is Mark S. Granovetter's "The Strength of Weak Ties," *American Journal of Sociology* 78, no. 6 (May 1973): 1360–80.

7. See, for example, Duncan Watts, *Small Worlds: The Science of a Connected Age* (W. W. Norton, 2004).

8. Ronald S. Burt, "The Social Origins of Good Ideas," manuscript, October 2002, www.analytictech.com/mb709/readings/burt_SOGI.pdf. Clay Shirky describes Burt's research in his book *Here Comes Everybody: The Power of Organizing Without Organizations* (Penguin Books, 2009).

9. Karim R. Lakhani, Lars Bo Jeppesen, Peter A. Lohse, and Jill A. Panetta, "The

Value of Openness in Scientific Problem Solving," Harvard Business School Working Paper Number 07-050, January 2007.

10. Brian Uzzi and Jarrett Spiro, "Collaboration and Creativity: The Small World Problem," *American Journal of Sociology* 111, no. 2 (September 2005): 447–504. This research was brought to popular awareness by Jonah Lehrer's article "Groupthink: The Brainstorming Myth," *New Yorker*, January 30, 2012.

11. Interview with Kevin Blue, November 7, 2011.

12. See, for example, Daniel Kahneman, *Thinking, Fast and Slow* (Farrar, Straus and Giroux, 2011).

13. David Rock, "Managing with the Brain in Mind," *strategy+business* 56 (Autumn 2009): 4.

14. Interview with Andrew Blau, October 10, 2011.

15. Ronald Heifetz and Martin Linksy, *Leadership on the Line: Staying Alive Through the Dangers of Leading* (Harvard Business School Press, 2002).

16. Interview with Neil Grimmer, January 25, 2012. See the Introduction for more details on this story.

17. In her book *Mind in the Making: The Seven Essential Life Skills Every Child Needs* (HarperCollins, 2010), Ellen Galinsky devotes a chapter to the development of perspective-taking skills among children, drawing on brain-science research by Rebecca Saxe at MIT, among others. See, for example, Saxe's article (with Susan Carey and Nancy Kanwisher), "Understanding Other Minds: Linking Developmental Psychology and Functional Neuroimaging," *Annual Review of Psychology* 55 (2004): 87–124.

FRAME THE ISSUES

1. Christopher Chabris and Daniel Simons, *Invisible Gorilla: How Our Intuitions Deceive Us* (Three Rivers Press, 2011).

2. The term *curse of knowledge* was originally coined by Robin Hogwarth in Colin Camerer, George Loewenstein, and Mark Weber, "The Curse of Knowledge in Economic Settings: An Experimental Analysis," *Journal of Political Economy*, 1989. It was later popularized in Chip and Dan Heath's *Made to Stick: Why Some Ideas Survive and Others Die* (Random House, 2007).

3. http://hbr.org/2007/12/breakthrough-thinking-from-inside-the-box; shar/1.

4. A number of authors have pointed out the power of thinking inside different boxes, including Kevin P. Coyne, Patricia Gorman Clifford, and Renée Dye, "Breakthrough Thinking from Inside the Box," *Harvard Business Review*, December 2007, 70–78; Barry Nalebuff and Ian Ayres, *Why Not?: How to Use Everyday Ingenuity to Solve Problems Big and Small* (Harvard Business Review

Press, 2006); and Drew Boyd and Jacob Goldenberg, *Inside the Box: A Proven System of Creativity for Breakthrough Results* (Simon & Schuster, 2013).

5. Interviews with Diane Rosenberg, Terry Lee, Lana Guernsey, and Grace Voorhis, October 9, 2012.

6. Popular business memes taken from bestselling books: Clayton Christensen, *Innovator's Dilemma: The Revolutionary Book That Will Change the Way You Do Business* (HarperBusiness, 2011); W. Chan Kim and Renee Mauborgne, *Blue Ocean Strategy: How to Create Uncontested Market Space and Make Competition Irrelevant* (Harvard Business Review Press, 2005); Malcolm Gladwell, *The Tipping Point: How Little Things Can Make a Big Difference* (Bay Back Books, 2002); and Robert Kaplan and David Norton, *The Balanced Scorecard: Translating Strategy into Action* (Harvard Business Review Press, 1996).

7. Hagerty details gathered from interviews with Erik Okerstrom (January 5, 2012) and Jonathan Star and Susan Stickley (January 4, 2012).

8. Interview with Michael Schrage, October 3, 2011.

SET THE SCENE

1. Interview with Darcy Draft, November 16, 2012.

2. Interview with Corey Ford, October 1, 2012.

3. L. Edwards and P. Torcellini, *A Literature Review on the Effects of Natural Light on Building Occupants* (US Department of Energy, National Renewable Energy Laboratory, 2002).

4. Ravi Mehta and Rui (Juliet) Zhu, "Blue or Red? Exploring the Effect of Color on Cognitive Task Performances," *Science* 323, no. 5918 (February 27, 2009): 1226–29. For a summary, see Pam Belluck, "Reinvent Wheel? Blue Room. Defusing a Bomb? Red Room," *New York Times*, February 5, 2009.

5. O. Seppanen, W. J. Fisk, and Q. H. Levi, "Room Temperature and Productivity in Office Work," presented to Healthy Buildings Conference 2006, Lawrence Berkeley National Laboratory Report #LBNL-60952.

6. Ravi Mehta, Rui (Juliet) Zhu, and Amar Cheema, "Is Noise Always Bad? Exploring the Effects of Ambient Noise on Creative Cognition," *Journal of Consumer Research* 3, no. 4 (December 2012): 784–99.

7. See MIT video about Building 20: http://mit150.mit.edu/multimedia/building-20-magical-incubator.

8. For an early telling of the Building 20 story—complete with pictures—see Stewart Brand's classic *How Buildings Learn: What Happens After They're Built* (Viking Penguin, 1994), 26–28. This story has also been retold by Steven Johnson in *Where Good Ideas Come From: The Natural History of Innovation* (River-

head, 2011), and by Jonah Lehrer in "Groupthink: The Brainstorming Myth," *New Yorker,* January 30, 2012.

9. Interviews with Darcy Draft (November 16, 2012) and Jonathan Star and Judy Cheng (October 26, 2012).

10. Interview with Gervais Tompkin, January 18, 2012.

11. Interview with Eamonn Kelly, July 12, 2012.

12. John Medina, *Brain Rules: 12 Principles for Surviving and Thriving at Work, Home and School* (Pear Press, 2008), 234.

13. Thanks to Dan Roam and Lynn Carruthers for help in thinking through this list of visual elements and how they relate to one another.

14. As shown in the diagram on page 48, the nine elements of the Business Model Generation Canvas are key partners, key resources, key activities, cost structure, value propositions, customer segments, customer relationships, channels, and revenue streams.

15. Interview with Alexander Osterwalder, October 29, 2012.

16. Insights about the strategic value of graphic recording gathered from interviews with Lynn Carruthers (September 11, 2012), Emily Shepard (September 18, 2012), and David Sibbet (December 19, 2012). To learn about graphic recording and other visual techniques, see the website of the International Forum of Visual Practitioners, http://ifvpcommunity.ning.com/, or the Grove, http://www.grove.com.

17. Interview with Gretchen Gscheidle, November 9, 2012.

18. Interview with Dan Roam, August 17, 2012.

19. See Edwin Hutchins, *Cognition in the Wild* (A Bradford Book, 1996).

20. Interviews with Gervais Tompkin (October 21, 2011, and January 18, 2012) and Amanda Ramos (March 8, 2012).

21. Shai Danziger, Jonathan Levav, and Liora Avniam-Pesso, "Extraneous Factors in Judicial Decisions," *PNAS* 108, no. 17 (2011): 6889–92; published ahead of print April 11, 2011, http://www.pnas.org/content/early/2011/03/29/1018033108 .short. For a summary of this academic article, see Binyamin Applebaum, "Up for Parole? Better Hope You're First on the Docket," *New York Times,* April 14, 2011.

22. Interview with Bernie Jaworski, March 1, 2012.

23. Interview with Darcy Draft, November 16, 2012.

MAKE IT AN EXPERIENCE

1. Daniel Schacter, *The Seven Sins of Memory: How the Mind Forgets and Remembers* (Mariner Books, 2002).

2. With one simple step, you might never "lose" your glasses again. Here's the tip:

when putting them down somewhere, just say out loud to yourself, "I am putting my glasses on the coffee table." By doing this, the information will now be encoded in your brain and it's almost guaranteed you'll remember where they are later. (You're welcome!)

3.   See Carl Wieman, "Why Not Try a Scientific Approach to Science Education?" *Science*, September–October 2007.

4.   See Emily Hanford, "Physicists Seek to Lose the Lecture as Teaching Tool," National Public Radio, January 1, 2012, http://www.npr.org/2012/01/01/144550920/physicists-seek-to-lose-the-lecture-as-teaching-tool.

5.   Ina Fried, "Interview: Brad Smith on Transforming Intuit into a Mobile-First Company," *All Things Digital*, online publication (Dow Jones & Company), June 26, 2012, http://allthingsd.com/20120626/interview-brad-smith-on-transforming-intuit-into-a-mobile-first-company/).

6.   Details from Intuit taken from interviews with Kaaren Hanson (December 19, 2011, and February 21, 2012) and Joseph O'Sullivan (September 21, 2012).

7.   Malcolm Gladwell, *Blink: The Power of Thinking Without Thinking* (Back Bay Books, 2007). To learn how human intuition works in practice, check out two fine books by the research psychologist Gary Klein: *The Power of Intuition* and *Sources of Power*. Also, for a valuable overview of the scientific arguments and evidence about when it is—and isn't—a good idea to go with your gut, see Daniel Kahneman and Gary Klein, "Conditions for Intuitive Expertise: A Failure to Disagree," *American Psychologist* 64, no. 6 (September 2009): 515–26.

8.   According to Damasio, speaking at an Aspen Institute event, the first major symposium on the scientific study of human emotion was held in 1995, hosted by the Society for Neuroscience (see http://fora.tv/2009/07/04/Antonio_Damasio_This_Time_With_Feeling).

9.   A leading theory, proposed by Damasio, is the "somatic marker hypothesis," which posits the role of our emotions in decision-making is to tag ideas with judgments (as "good" or "bad," for example), thereby facilitating recall and processing. While some support for this theory comes from brain imaging and behavioral experiments, research to better understand these mechanisms is ongoing.

10. Donald A. Norman, *The Design of Everyday Things* (Basic Books, 2002).

11. Data on the De La Salle Christian Brothers taken from the institution's website on June 21, 2013, http://www.lasalle.org/en/who-are-we/statistics/.

12. Story captured from interviews with David Hawke (February 28, 2012), Ambrose Payne (March 3, 2012), and Michael Mulcany and Joe McCrossen (February 15, 2012).

13. Freytag's arc is referenced in B. Joseph Pine II and James H. Gimore, *The Experience Economy*, updated ed. (Harvard Business Press, 2011); and Nancy Duarte, *Resonate: Present Visual Stories That Transform Audiences* (Wiley, 2010).

14. Syd Field, *Screenplay*, rev. ed. (Delta, 2005).

15. Duarte, *Resonate.*

16. Jeanne Liedtka, "Strategy as Experienced," *Rotman*, Winter 2011, 30.

CONFRONTING THE "YABBUTS"

1. Frans de Waal, *Chimpanzee Politics: Power and Sex among Apes*, 25th anniversary ed. (Johns Hopkins University Press, 2007).

2. Ibid., 197.

3. Art Kleiner, *Who Really Matters: The Core Group Theory of Power, Privilege, and Success* (Currency/Doubleday, 2003).

4. Bob Frisch's book *Who's in the Room* also discusses this phenomenon at length. Frisch observes that most organizations operate officially under "the myth of the top team" while being informally run by "teams with no names," which consist of Kleiner's core group plus their informal advisers.

5. Peter Schwartz, *Learnings from the Long View* (CreateSpace Independent Publishing Platform, 2011).

6. Felix Gillette, "The Rise and Inglorious Fall of MySpace," *Bloomberg Businessweek*, June 21, 2011.

7. Yinka Adegoke, "Special Report: How News Corp. Got Lost in MySpace," Reuters, April 7, 2011; Brian Stelter, "News Corporation Sells MySpace for $35 Million," *New York Times*, Media Decoder blog, June 29, 2011.

8. Alfred Rappaport, *Saving Capitalism from Near-Termism* (McGraw-Hill, 2011).

9. Interview with Peter Johnson, April 11, 2012.

10. For a good overview of this famous experiment—and its aftermath—see Jonah Lehrer, "Don't! The Secret of Self-Control," *New Yorker*, May 18, 2009; or Ellen Galinsky, *Mind in the Making: The Seven Essential Skills Every Child Needs* (William Morrow Paperbacks, 2010).

11. Malcolm Gladwell, *Outliers: The Story of Success* (Back Bay Books, 2011); Geoff Colvin, *Talent Is Overrated: What Really Separates World-Class Performers from Everybody Else* (Portfolio Trade, 2010). Yo-Yo Ma started playing cello at age four according to his official online biography at http://www.yo-yoma.com/yo-yo-ma-biography.

12. For a review of the literature on overconfidence, see Daniel Kahneman, *Thinking, Fast and Slow* (Farrar, Straus and Giroux, 2011).

13. Interview with Ellen Goldman (April 3, 2012).

14. See Ellen Goldman, "Experiences That Develop the Ability to Think Strategically," *Journal of Healthcare Management* 54, no. 6 (November/December 2009): 403–17.

15. For one definition of "strategic thinking" and its elements that informed our list, see Ellen F. Goldman, "Strategic Thinking at the Top," *MIT Sloan Management Review* 48, no. 4 (Summer 2007): 75–81.

16. See Shane Greenstein and Michelle Devereux, "The Crisis at Encyclopaedia Britannica," Kellogg School of Management case study #5-306-504, revised July 28, 2009. Full disclosure: Chris's first job out of college was as a staff writer and editor on the fifteenth revised edition of *Encyclopaedia Britannica* in the mid-1980s, when the firm was still in its heyday. In more recent years, Britannica has repositioned itself as a provider of curriculum products for schools (both print and digital) with some success.

17. Gabriel García Márquez, *Chronicle of a Death Foretold*, repr. ed. (Vintage, 2003).

18. Niccolò Machiavelli, *The Prince*, trans. and with an introduction by Harvey C. Mansfield, 2nd ed. (University of Chicago Press, 1998), 23–24.

19. Interview with John Seely Brown, November 10, 2011.

MAKE *YOUR* MOMENT

1. See www.thegiin.org.

2. JP Morgan, "Impact Investments: An Emerging Asset Class," *Global Research*, November 29, 2010. See also the report by the Monitor Institute "Investing for Social and Environmental Impact"; and Antony Bugg-Levine and Jed Emerson, *Impact Investing: Transforming How We Make Money While Making a Difference* (Jossey-Bass, 2011).

3. Details from the Rockefeller Foundation's Bellagio session and the aftermath were gathered from interviews with Katherine Fulton (November 4, 2011), Katherine Fulton and Jessica Freireich (February 28, 2012), Amit Bouri (March 12, 2012), and Antony Bugg-Levine (July 7, 2012).

4. Niccolò Machiavelli, *The Prince*, trans. and with an introduction by Harvey C. Mansfield, 2nd ed. (University of Chicago Press, 1998), 23–24.

ACKNOWLEDGMENTS

Many of the ideas in this book originate from an extraordinary place called Global Business Network (GBN), where we first met in 2001. GBN was a small shop with a big mission: to help organizations think more creatively and expansively about their biggest opportunities and challenges. From 1987 through 2012, GBN introduced scenario planning into hundreds of organizations of all kinds—and in doing so, shaped the way that thousands of leaders think about the future and make decisions. On a personal level, it was an amazing community of practitioners marked by ruthless curiosity, mutual respect, and a deep commitment to making the world a better place.

While GBN is gone, its legacy lives on. Scenario planning is today the most widely used tool for navigating future uncertainty, and the GBN diaspora continues to affect change across all kinds of organizations around the world. We feel lucky to be part of it.

Two fellow GBN alums played outsize roles in shaping this book. Jenny Johnston, GBN's former all-star senior editor, was by our side from the first draft proposal through the final galley edits—challenging us to be tighter in our reasoning and clearer in our expression, and working beyond the call of duty at critical crunch times. Nancy Murphy was our fearless maven and muse, who coached us at every step to make choices that would honor the content and serve the reader best.

Our agent, Christy Fletcher, saw the potential in this project early on and offered spot-on counsel throughout the process. She saved us precious time and energy, keeping us focused on what mattered most.

We had fantastic support from the editorial team at Simon & Schuster. Ben Loehnen's keen eye for story, tone, and consistency elevated the book's coherence and impact. Brit Hvide patiently shepherded us through the process, often navigating new territory to help execute our vision. We're also grateful to Emily Loose, who saw the initial vision of the proposal—and then tactfully tore up our original outline and replaced it with one we would actually deliver.

Christopher Simmons and Nathan Sharp, of the San Francisco design firm MINE, created an elegant visual identity for the book and were invaluable thought partners in helping us hone our core ideas to the level of clarity that's required to find expression in simple images.

Finally, this book would not exist if not for the 100+ professionals who gave generously of their time, ideas, and stories through often lengthy interviews. Although it pained us to leave some great stuff on the cutting room floor, every one of these discussions advanced our understanding in important ways. We tried our best to listen deeply to the diverse perspectives of these remarkable people, and hope that we have done them justice here.

FROM CHRIS ERTEL

The convention in movie credits is that the big stars come first. In book acknowledgments, they often come last. I think the movie people have it right.

My mother and father—both professional book editors—gave me the gift of daily encouragement, relentless curiosity, and a deep love of words. Well into her eighties today, my mother managed to find a few dozen edits in a near-final manuscript that we'd somehow missed in numerous rounds of rewrites. As *Moments of Impact* goes to press, I can feel the warmth of my dad's proud smile from far away.

To say that my wife, Johanna Buurman, was "supportive" of this work would be an absurd understatement. By the time we were excited about the idea for this book but not yet sure we could pull it off, Johanna made it clear that I had no choice but to take the leap and just do it. Our daughter Vera was too young to understand why Dad was going to the café instead of the office every day for a year. But she sensed I could use some help, and put Gigi—one of her favorite stuffies—in my bag each morning to keep a smile on my face while writing.

Where would we be without mentors? My close friend and co-conspirator Eamonn Kelly threw his body and soul behind this work, propelling it onward in countless ways over several years. Some debts are too big to pay back; this one I can only pay forward.

Whenever I felt stuck on content, three names were at the top of my speed dial list. Brie Linkenhoker schooled me in cognitive science and behavioral economics in ways that inform every chapter. Jonathan Star was my reliable acid test for the expert practitioner audience; his critiques made several chapters stronger. And Napier Collyns—a master networker who has coaxed many worthy books into existence—helped connect this one to the deeper currents of intellectual history it rides upon.

A few big brains have dug especially deep grooves in mine in ways that helped shape this work, notably Stewart Brand, Joe Fuller, Katherine Fulton, Joel Garreau, Gene Hammel, Ronald Heifetz, Larry Keeley, Art Kleiner, Jay Ogilvy, Anno Saxenian, Michael Schrage, Clay Shirky, Peter Schwartz, Kees van der Heijden, Steve Weber, and Lawrence Wilkinson.

I've been fortunate to learn with and from scores of "black belt" designers of strategic conversation over the years. If you ever get a chance to work with any of these people, jump at it: Sartaz Ahmed, Andrew Blau, Nicole Boyer, Jim Butcher, Lynn Carruthers, Judy Cheng, Kristin Cobble, John ("JC") Collins, Mick Costigan, Don Derosby, Angelo Frigo, Bernie Jaworski, Katie Joyce, Erik Kiaer, Barbara Kibbe, Pete Leyden, Sophia Liang, Matt Locsin,

Matt Marcus, Joe McCrossen, Michael Mulcahy, Enrique Ortegon, Steve Pickle, Ryan Pikkel, Matt Ranen, Chris Riley, Diana Scearce, Erik Smith, Karin Stawarky, and Susan Stickley.

As a consultant, I've also been lucky to team up with some great clients who pushed me to do my best work, including Laura Campbell, David Hawke, Andy Hines, David Klinginsmith, Ambrose Payne, and Maryln Walton. Several friends and colleagues also made valuable contributions along the way, including Mel Blake, Jenny Collins, Emma Ginger, Ron Lieber, Bill Murphy, Melissa Quinn, and Rogerio Rizzi.

Finally, a number of close friends have stuck with me through the decades in good times and bad, lifting my spirits while always challenging me to be true to myself. Here's to you guys: John Mayer, Karen Levesque and Matt Schwartz, and TJ Tedesco.

FROM LISA KAY SOLOMON

I'm fortunate to be surrounded by a community of amazing, supportive, and inspirational people who helped bring this book to life.

This book would not have happened without Chuck House, professional instigator, remarkable thought leader, and the one and only winner of the Hewlett Packard Medal of Defiance. It was Chuck who gave Chris and me our first audience to present our shared passion for designing strategic conversations at a Stanford Media X conference in 2010. From there, a book mission was born.

Business model pioneers Alex Osterwalder and Yves Pigneur and their talented designer Alan Smith co-created the book *Business Model Generation* (BMG); it has had a profound impact on the world and especially on me. Their work made me want to become an author to help empower leaders with new tools for today's complex realities. Patrick van der Pijl, BMG's producer, has been a tireless advocate of this project, as well as a brilliant creative collaborator and dear friend.

When you believe, as I do, that design has the power to change the world, it helps to be part of an extended community that believes the same thing. My colleagues at the DMBA program at California College of the Arts—Nathan Shedroff, Susan Worthman, and Tim Smith—along with my students constantly teach me to be a better practitioner of the craft. I'm particularly grateful to DMBA alum Michelle Dawson, whose research, design, and production help, along with her boundless enthusiasm, proved invaluable to this book.

I also want to thank the many brave "boundary crossers" who inspire me to experiment on the edges and have the courage to do things differently. People like Dan Roam, Jeanne Liedtka, Nancy Duarte, David Kelley, Daniel Pink, Adam Grant, Sara Beckman, Kaaren Hanson, Diane Rosenberg, Kim Saxe, Heather McLeod Grant, Corey Ford, Kevin Blue, Jennifer Dulski, Dave Viotti, JD Schramm, Carole Robin, Ricardo Levy, Ken Bogdanoff, Phil Wickham, Bill Tobin, and Erik van der Pluijm. Each of these remarkable people, in their own way, is trying to catalyze a movement through human-centered design.

And then there are my own personal sages—friends and colleagues who have never tired of asking about the project, reviewing early passages, and providing loving and constructive feedback. Huge thanks to Alison Wagonfeld, Ed Batista, Randi Caplan, Adene Sacks, Ann Green, Laura Lauder, Robbie Baxter, Hildy Agustin, Tracy Tefertiller, Katharine Moir, Julie Clugage, Leslie Bull, Carolyn Heller, Lynn Carruthers, Emily Shepard, Anthony Weeks, Ching-Yee Hu, Karen Pace, Aliza Gazek, Kelly Vicars, and Sara Leslie.

They say that you can't take Philadelphia out of the girl, and I'm so grateful for my East Coast posse who helped me "keep it real" throughout the writing of this book: Jennifer Finkelstein, Melanie Kaplan, Jennifer Koen, Melissa Libow, Rae Ringel, and Rachel Schwartz.

I don't think this book would have happened without my mother, Bonnie Kay, a systems thinking executive coach who taught me early on that "the only thing worse than having the conversation is *not* having the conversation." Her generosity of spirit and philosophical influence can be found throughout these pages. My father, Michael Kay, listened to my ideas for this book with humor, humility, and endless patience—qualities he embodies and has taught me to live by. I also want to thank my extended family of caring supporters who sweetly understood that it was time to stop asking, "Is it done yet?"

My husband, Glenn, gets to have more strategic conversations with me than just about anyone (not always designed, I might add). Throughout this process, he has been an unwavering advocate and source of strength. As my confidant, built-in tennis coach, and amazing dad to our kids, he's far surpassed the "good to great" model for life partners. Our two girls, Tobey and Samantha, light up my every day with their reminders to be both silly and serious, playful and intentional, cooperative and independent—also great lessons for our toughest strategic moments. Mostly I'm grateful for the morning kisses and evening snuggles that put even the most difficult strategic conversation into perspective.

INTERVIEW LIST

We're grateful to everyone that gave their time to help create *Moments of Impact.*

Enrique Allen

Chris Ballinger

Ephi Banaynal dela Cruz

Ed Batista

Sara Beckman

Robin Beers

Scott Belsky

Becky Bermont

Andrew Blau

Kevin Blue

George Borst

Randall Borud

Amit Bouri

David Bradford

Erin Bradford

John Seely Brown

Amy Buckner Chowdhry

Antony Bugg-Levine

Ann Bybee

Stuart Candy

Marcelo Cardoso

Lynn Carruthers

Lisa Chen

Judy Cheng

Kristin Cobble

Napier Collyns

Chip Conley

Lou Cove

Stuart Davidson

Don Derosby

Scott Doorley

Darcy Draft

Nancy Duarte

Carl Engle

Tom Fishburne

Corey Ford

Andreas Forsland

Jessica Freireich

Joe Fuller

Katherine Fulton

Lisa Gansky

Laura Garcia-Manrique

Ian Gee

James Gilmore

Jesse Goldhammer

Ellen Goldman

Jason Green

Neil Grimmer

Gretchen Gscheidle

Lana Guernsey

Ron Guerrier

Chris Hacker

Kaaren Hanson

David Hawke

Ronald Heifetz

Chris Hood

Chuck House

Ching-Yee Hu

Bernie Jaworski

Steve Jennings

Peter Johnson

Larry Keeley

Eamonn Kelly

Barbara Kibbe

Art Kleiner

Clint Korver

Terry Lee

Ricardo Levy

Jeanne Liedtka

Brie Linkenhoker

Bob Lurie

John Maeda

Roger Martin

Jason Mayden

Heather McLeod Grant

Joe McCrossen

Chris Meyer

Robin Mockenhaupt

Bill Moggridge

Tom Mulhern

Michael Mulcahy

Joseph O'Sullivan

Eric Okerstrom

Enique Ortegon

Alex Osterwalder

Ambrose Payne

Steve Pickle

Amanda Ramos

Matt Ranen

Chris Riley

Dan Roam

Carole Robin

Diane Rosenberg

Diana Scearce

Michael Schrage

Peter Schwartz

Ben Seesel

Jeff Semenchuck

Nathan Shedroff

Emily Shepard

Clay Shirky

David Sibbet

Allen Smith

Erik Smith

Levin Somaya

Jonathan Star

Karin Stawarky

Susan Stickley

Gervais Tompkin

Patrick Van der Pijl

Grace Voorhis

Julia Wada

Alison Wagonfeld

Steve Weber

Phil Wickham

Scott Witthoft

Lawrence Wilkinson

Joon Yun

Pavel Zamudio-Ramirez

INDEX